D0867489

Jon M. Sweeney is a writer, editor, retreat leader and popular speaker. He was the featured speaker at Washington National Cathedral in Washington, DC, in 2004 on the feast day of St Francis of Assisi.

He is best known as the author of books that present key people, events, and legends of the Middle Ages to a wide audience. SPCK published his book, *Light in the Dark Ages: The Friendship of Francis and Clare of Assisi*, which was selected in the USA by both the History Book Club and Book-of-the-Month Club. He is also the author of *Strange Heaven*, a study of the traditions relating to the Virgin Mary; *Praying with Our Hands*, published by Wild Goose in the UK; *The Road to Assisi*, an edited version of Paul Sabatier's classic biography of St Francis (more than 40,000 copies sold); and the forthcoming, *Cloister Talks: What I Have Learned from My Friends the Monks* (Brazos).

For many years, Jon was the co-founder and editor-in-chief of SkyLight Paths Publishing, a multifaith trade book publisher in Vermont. Since 2004, he has been the associate publisher at Paraclete Press in Massachusetts.

He also writes book and film reviews, and author interviews, for the popular website, www.explorefaith.org; and for magazines such as *Catholic Digest* and the *Lutheran*. He is one of the contributors to the popular daily devotional, *Daily Guideposts*. Jon worships at St James' Episcopal Church in Woodstock, Vermont, and was appointed by his bishop in 2006 to the Committee on Discernment for the Diocese of Vermont.

BEAUTY AWAKENING BELIEF

*How the medieval worldview
inspires faith today*

Jon M. Sweeney

Morehouse Publishing

NEW YORK · HARRISBURG · DENVER

First published in Great Britain in 2009 by

Society for Promoting Christian Knowledge, 36 Causton Street, London SW1P 4ST

First published in North America in 2009 by

Morehouse Publishing, 4775 Linglestown Road, Harrisburg, PA 17112

Morehouse Publishing, 445 Fifth Avenue, New York, NY 10016

Morehouse Publishing is an imprint of Church Publishing Incorporated.

Library of Congress Cataloging-in-Publication Data

A catalog record for this book is available from the Library of Congress.

Typeset by Graphicraft Ltd, Hong Kong
Printed in Great Britain by Ashford Colour Press
Produced on paper from sustainable forests

09 10 11 12 13 14   10 9 8 7 6 5 4 3 2 1

For Brendan, fellow traveller

The dull mind rises to truth through that which is material
And, in seeing this light, is resurrected
(Abbot Suger, written on the gilded main doors
of the Abbey Church of St-Denis)

Contents

Acknowledgements   xi

1 The worldview of the Gothic cathedral   1

2 Inviting God in: space   11

3 Making our places holy: sanctuary   25

4 A place that is cool: stone   39

5 Open your eyes and see: light   55

6 Learning to live with the light off: darkness   67

7 Don't take yourself too seriously: gargoyles   79

8 Reaching to heaven: flying buttresses   89

9 Beauty awakens belief   99

Notes   111

Acknowledgements

It was Coleridge who coined the term 'library cormorant' for those of us who live off old books for our sustenance. One of the pleasures of writing this book, in contrast to others I have done, was that it involved less library time, and more travel and conversation with good friends. Of course, there are still many books credited in the Notes – too many, probably, for the reader of typical patience – but I must also say that conversations with friends, and Brendan Walsh in particular, were a real pleasure.

Henry Adams wrote in *Mont Saint Michel and Chartres* about the imagery of Christ in the portal doorways of Chartres Cathedral: 'Before 1200, the Church seems not to have felt the need of appealing habitually to terror; the promise of hope and happiness was enough.' He continues a couple of sentences later, 'A hundred years later, every church portal [built subsequent to Chartres] showed Christ not as Savior but as Judge' (p. 70). As Adams showed so clearly, the humanity of Chartres shines through even today. My hope is that, in this book, I have successfully captured for the reader the ways in which both the Abbey Church of Mont St-Michel and Chartres Cathedral captured the Gothic moments, and then, how we might recapture the same.

All quotations from the Bible are taken from the New Revised Standard Version, used by permission. Quotations from Dante's *Paradiso* are taken from the classic translation of Henry Wadsworth Longfellow.

1

The worldview of the Gothic cathedral

For as men think, so do they build.
(Joann Herder)[1]

Imagine it is the year 1400, and you are visiting Chartres Cathedral for the first time. You have never before seen a faithful reproduction, or even heard an oral description, of this truly remarkable structure, which dominates the busy, dirty, commercial city and the countryside for miles around. Climbing up the Rue du Borg on foot you enter the cathedral itself, and find yourself in a cavernous space, illuminated by the flickering light of hundreds of candles rebounding off exquisitely beautiful stained-glass windows. Though greatly moved by your surroundings, you do not find it at all difficult to understand or 'read' the cathedral: on the contrary, it is quite clear to you how it wordlessly communicates the Christian story.

* * *

The hidden meanings of great cathedrals like Chartres, Mont St-Michel and the Abbey Church of St-Denis were once plain to our ancestors. It is those meanings that I hope to tease out in the pages that follow, so that the spirituality of these enormous, ornate, extravagantly expensive, towering sacred spaces – and the vision of the medieval architects and builders who constructed them – might refresh and inspire our faith today.

The Scriptures tell of divine order in the universe. The verse from the Apocrypha, 'But you have arranged all things by measure and number and weight' (Wisdom of Solomon 11.20), was made famous by St Augustine throughout the medieval world, and most theologians of the time believed that God arranges all things down to the finest detail. The Gothic builders took this to heart in creating forms they believed corresponded to the order of the cosmos and to the Godhead. The vision portrayed inside a great cathedral is the vision thought to come directly from the heavens. Beauty was to be brought out in order, never disorder, as the medieval architect laboured to discover the secrets of the God of ultimate design.

Gothic cathedrals usually follow what is called a cruciform plan, that is, shaped like a cross (though this is not exclusive to the Gothic style), with the longer axis running from west to east. The cathedral faces east, towards the rising sun and Jerusalem, where Christ was risen, and it is in the east end of the church that the altar is located. At the west end of that axis is the front door. The shorter axis, running south to north, forms the 'arms' of the cross, which are called the transepts: they are located towards the front of the building, between the nave – the central portion of any church – and the choir and chancel (the steps leading up to the sanctuary and altar). Running along the sides of the nave of most Gothic churches, perpendicular to that longer west–east axis, are one or two aisles, and all along those aisles, columns.

The central focus of Gothic design was always the incarnate God in Christ, rather than the Trinity, the Godhead, or the person of God the Father. We might say that the Gothic architect took his primary inspiration from the opening

phrase of the Gospel of John, 'In the beginning was the Word.'
As one scholar has expressed it:

> [W]here the created and the uncreated, the natural and
> the supernatural, the eternal and the historical came
> together, is where Christ was situated, as God made
> man. He was 'light born of light,' yet was made of solid
> flesh. Ever since the building of Saint-Denis [the first
> Gothic church], Gothic art had strained to express the
> incarnation.[2]

At the Mass, a medieval Christian would have felt open to
the glories of heaven at that moment in that place, and no
less profoundly than if a giant hand had reached down from
the clouds – but the One acting upon him was a loving Jesus.
A Christian's 'bread of heaven' was found only on the high
altar, there.

Medieval spirituality was both more credulous and more
embodied than our own. For the medieval person, a symbol was an objective piece of reality: it *was* that very thing
it represented. An image of Christ or the Virgin in the form
of an icon, or a fresco, or a sculpture was a very portal to
Jesus or Mary. The builders of the first Gothic cathedrals had
been taught by the philosopher John Scotus Eriugena – one
of the finest minds of the early medieval period – that a piece
of stone may only be understood for what it really is, if we
see God in it. The materials they used were thus transformed in their hands: the slab of marble forming the high
altar of a cathedral would be regarded as the very stone upon
which Abraham had been willing to offer Isaac, or as the place
where sacrifices were made in the temple during Jesus' time
or, most importantly, Calvary, where Christ offered himself
for the salvation of the world.

In the chapters that follow we will focus on seven essential words of medieval spirituality: 'space', 'sanctuary', 'stone',
'light', 'darkness', 'grotesques' and 'flight'.

* * *

This style of architecture was not originally called *Gothic*. In fact, *Gothic* originated as an implied criticism. We don't know the precise origin of the term, as it was applied to arising architectural styles in northern Europe, but we do know that it must have originally been used as a term of reproach. Gothic means 'of the Goths', a barbarian people who had stood in stark contrast to the humanism and civilization of the Romans during the waning of the Roman Empire. All things *Gothic* were being compared to a nomadic tribe that invaded the West. Renaissance-era Italian critics, touting the virtues of their *own* era, coined the term as a pejorative. They intended to compare the barbarians, the Goths, to the 'barbaric' art that had begun in the Middle Ages.

The term survives today, in part, because it actually predates the word *medieval,* which means 'the middle age'. The people of the Renaissance also coined *medieval* as a way of naming the era that stood between the classical era and their own. It also was something of a dismissal. That millennium of faith (from roughly AD 400 to 1400) and perspective was believed to be of little value, since they did not continue many of the artistic forms and styles of antiquity. And they used words such as 'ignorant' and 'monstrous' to describe the style of architecture that sits like a signpost on the timeline between the classical and the Renaissance. Alexander Pope expresses the attitude best when he writes these lines:

> A second Deluge Learning thus o'er-run,
> And the Monks finish'd what the Goths begun.

At least since about the late eighteenth century – with the beginning of the neo-Gothic revival in Europe – those who appreciate the pointed style have been more willing to call it *Gothic.* But it is only in the last century that a fresh understanding of the Middle Ages has begun to permeate university curricula and, even so, it has not really trickled down into popular culture. Popular films and novels are still made on the backs of medieval abbeys where monks bludgeon themselves in penitence, and schoolchildren still learn about this era by means of books that focus on the gruesome and the bizarre. I'm thinking, for example, of the popular Horrible Histories series of books that use cartoon to focus young readers on the most horrible and strangest aspects of what life was like in the medieval (and other) eras. They are entertaining – very entertaining, in fact – and they encourage kids to read about history, but of course they also leave them thinking about the Middle Ages in the way that most educated adults think about the era: full of 'horrible history'.

There is more to the story than just that. The truth is that the twelfth and thirteenth centuries, which provided the environment for the growth of the Gothic, were not as violent as was the twentieth. There were renaissances of learning and art and craft and workers' rights in the early eleventh, thirteenth, fourteenth and fifteenth centuries. There were periods of time when the churches were almost completely corrupt, and for many years or generations on end those who were clearly corrupt got away with their sins. But there was also great beauty, creativity and simplicity to life in the Middle Ages that resulted in a high level of quality in life.

* * *

Gothic cathedrals usually defy the typical guidebook. Famous religious buildings usually have guidebooks to show you around, and these books give you the history of the church ('Why is this one supposed to be important?'), the height, width and purpose of some of the more notable features ('How tall is that window?'), and they sometimes explain some of the deeper meanings of the things you have come to look at ('Why is there a lion beside that man, while that other man seems to be holding a griddle?'). Guide-books for religious buildings may tell you how to identify a minaret, or a pantocrator icon, where the *bimah* is located in a synagogue, or who built a chapel and when, but in the case of the great cathedrals they rarely give an understand-ing of why things matter and what role they play in the story of Christian faith.

I have visited hundreds of religious buildings in my life, from Orthodox churches with elaborate iconostases to mosques in city centres that don't even really look like mosques from the outside. I've sat in silence in a Quaker meet-ing house and I've been to services at a downtown synagogue. I was brought up in Baptist churches without adornment of any kind, but today I feel more at home with more 'Catholic' worship that feeds the senses.

Every place of worship is unique and each is intended to 'say' something about the way that God is understood, worshipped and alive. Every church building is intentional – it has been designed and built to spark some sort of reac-tion in you when you are in it, or even as you approach it. No building is neutral, and if you usually look for the great churches in the cities that you visit, you are already responding to what the builders long ago programmed into those structures. They are already speaking to you, even if in muffled tones. If you find yourself intrigued by the Gothic style, but also perhaps somewhat perplexed by it, all the better. What is a great Gothic church supposed to mean? I aim to explore this question in its many details and more subtle meanings.

Along the way, I hope to explain some interesting details. I will explain why you are likely to see a variety of art styles and architecture, spanning many centuries, combined in the same Gothic cathedral. I will explain why images such as those of pelicans and eagles appear over and over again, sometimes even on the pulpit. I will explain why Gothic stained-glass windows tend to be the largest of all styles of church window, and are positioned higher than others on the vaulted walls around the transepts and the chancel. I will explain certain details of those windows, and I will explain how relics of the saints, from body parts to pieces of clothing, are right at home in the same buildings that include sometimes frightening figures looking down on you as you walk in through the front door.

* * *

We don't build great Gothic churches much any more. Our worldview is different from the one that inspired the people of the High Middle Ages to do worship in the ways that they did. But just like today, not everyone was of the same opinion back then. There were those, for instance, who disagreed with the 'ostentation' and expense of Gothic buildings. What sorts of arguments were made long ago *against* building them, and how are those arguments echoed, today? What has changed in our worldview, from then to now, that makes big churches seem even less necessary than they once were?

We have newer 'cathedrals' today that prove to be more popular than the older ones, and they are still generally made of stone and glass. They are places such as art museums, where one can also experience transcendence. The Metropolitan Museum in New York City, the Louvre in Paris, the National Gallery in London – these are all far more crowded on a Saturday afternoon or Sunday morning than are the city churches and monumental cathedrals nearby. We even replicate religious reverence before the paintings, gazing at them in the way that saints gaze at their crucifixes in those same paintings. We stand before works of art sometimes by ourselves, anonymously and pensively, or with others in conversation. Sometimes the visit to the museum becomes a full day out of the house, with lunch or dinner at a nice restaurant, just as I once did with my parents on a typical Sunday after a long church service. We may even tithe on our way in or out of the museum; a 'suggested donation' is often all that is required, and it feels good to offer one. And of course there are always gifts and postcards – substitute sacramentals, perhaps – to be had in the gift shop.

Other new 'cathedrals' are natural wonders such as Yosemite (California) and Kilimanjaro (Tanzania). There's no indoor exclusivity to religion, and more than ever before in history, there's the feeling among Christians that God is to be known, worshipped and experienced *outside* of the four walls of church. We often make pilgrimages to beautiful parts of creation with no less intensity than a Jew visiting the Western Wall, a Muslim on the hajj, or a Christian in a side chapel at Santa Croce in Florence. Unlike our ancestors, we get our spirituality in many places and in many ways that churches and cathedrals no longer seem to exclusively provide.

With organized religion meaning less in our private lives, our religious spaces have come to mean less, too. There are many people today, perhaps they are even in the majority, for whom the concept of sacred space is no longer compelling, or never was. Perhaps for the majority of those under the age of thirty, cathedrals mean little or nothing at all. They are largely vacant, mostly sentimental places. For some, to look upon the ancient ruins of what was once a great cathedral, such as England's Glastonbury Abbey, is the same as to look on the ruins of the Roman Forum – as a simple artefact of history.

For those who have grown up with religion in their lives and have left it, great cathedrals and abbeys mean something else: they may be symbols of power and wealth, reminding us of the ways that religion has excluded more than it has included over the course of time. One person's place of worship and communion is another person's symbol of privilege. In this light, a place such as Chartres Cathedral or Westminster Abbey may feel off-putting at best, or oppressive, at worst. I went to France to explore Gothic cathedrals in detail, and to discover the Gothic cathedrals of France is to be reminded of the decline of western Christianity, particularly since the days of the French Revolution (1789). One purpose of that people's revolution was to overthrow the authority of the Church, which had been at times, to put it kindly, oppressive. Great churches were usually repurposed to become other things – hay lofts; prisons; museums (as if Christianity lay only in the past); blacksmith shops, for making more battle armour – and still others were renamed, becoming 'temples to the Divine Being', or something along those lines. In many respects, that era does not feel so long ago. Smaller churches are often sold by their bishops or congregations today, sometimes even abandoned or repurposed into restaurants, shops or office space. It's inconceivable, isn't it, that this would or could happen to the great cathedrals that many of us know by name? Sometimes I'm not sure.

There's no question that there's something about great church buildings that is lost on us until we step into them again for the first time. An agnostic, Anglican-raised W. H. Auden, had just such an experience in the 1930s while in Spain during the Civil War:

> On arriving in Barcelona, I found as I walked through the city that all the churches were closed and there was not a priest to be seen. To my astonishment, this discovery left me profoundly shocked and disturbed. The feeling was far too intense to be the result of a mere liberal dislike of intolerance, the notion that it is wrong to stop people from doing what they like, even if it is

something silly like going to church. I could not escape acknowledging that, however I had consciously ignored and rejected the Church for sixteen years, the existence of churches and what went on in them had all the time been very important to me.[3]

The great cathedrals are still with us, waiting to be rediscovered. They are more than the sites of coronations, royal weddings, solemn remembrances, and masses for the dead famous – in fact, much more. Come and see.

2

Inviting God in: space

———•◆•———

When the earth totters, with all its inhabitants,
it is I who keep its pillars steady.

(Psalm 75.3)

It's almost impossible for a Christian to reflect on the meaning of the great cathedrals without also reflecting on the usefulness of such buildings in our own day. In every middle to large city throughout Europe and the Americas, there are still enormous, beautiful, Gothic-style churches and they are mostly empty. They are shells of what they once were. What does it say about us that we disuse, or simply don't use, these buildings much at all any more? These tourist spots have been made into a new kind of symbol that is deadened, more museum-like. Are the great cathedrals a symbol of the future (or the not-entirely-yet-realized present) of the Church itself?

I can only guess that the wonder that a place like Chartres Cathedral or the Abbey Church of Mont St-Michel inspires in me in the early twenty-first century would have been multiplied in the imagination of someone more than 600 years ago. After all, I have read books, lots of books, easily obtained, explaining every aspect of the place. And I had seen photographs before visiting the great church for the first time, and talked with friends who had made the trip before me. I may have even seen something on the History Channel years ago; I don't remember.

But in the Middle Ages it was easy to 'find' or 'feel' God in a religious space. It is difficult to imagine a parallel experience, today. Perhaps the Grand Canyon, the Egyptian Pyramids, or the Great Wall of China, which books and photos simply cannot capture. Or, imagine a child who stands at the railing only a few feet away from one of the precipitous drops of Niagara Falls for the first time. That child will feel awe without even trying. Her eyes will widen; she will step back for a moment; and then her parent will take her hand and tell her that it's okay to be a part, for a time, of this incredible place. This is analogous to the experience of standing in the space of a great cathedral long ago, and perhaps, for some, subconsciously, even today.

* * *

These great spaces were created to communicate many things about God. They were new temples of Solomon. But it is curious to recall the very first time that humans decided to build a great cathedral, and how God thwarted them.

Soon after the Flood, people began to gather together in one place and coordinate their efforts, combining their skills, and cooperating for the first time. To read the account in Genesis 11 today is almost to imagine inspiration for a United Nations that might actually work:

> Now the whole earth had one language and the same words. And as they migrated from the east, they came upon a plain in the land of Shinar and settled there. And they said one to another, 'Come, let us make bricks, and burn them thoroughly.' And they had brick for stone, and bitumen for mortar.
>
> Then they said, 'Come, let us build ourselves a city, and a tower with its top in the heavens, and let us make

a name for ourselves; otherwise we shall be scattered abroad upon the face of the whole earth.'

(Genesis 11.1–4)

Why would God frown on this sort of cooperation? According to the story, Babel was the first city, as well as the first towering building, of the post-Flood world. The tower aimed to reach the heavens – just like the cathedrals of the medieval era – and yet, the builders said, 'Let us make us a name for ourselves.' The Tower of Babel was not created for the glory of God.

Later in the Hebrew Bible, we witness the construction of the Temple of Solomon. This great structure was built in tenth-century BC Jerusalem, and quickly became famous throughout the world of that era. In Judaism it is known as the First Temple, and was built in Jerusalem because King David made the city the centre of the Jewish kingdom. It was in Jerusalem where Abraham had offered his son, Isaac, centuries earlier, and so it would be there that the new kingdom and the First Temple would be built by David's son, King Solomon. The First Temple sat on the spot that is today the home of the Temple Mount in Jerusalem. The great structure stood there for nearly five centuries until the Babylonians razed it to the ground on the orders of King Nebuchadnezzar II in about 586 BC.

Solomon's Temple was a sight to see, as well as a temptation to attack. Rival kings throughout the era led raids on it, according to the biblical books of Kings and Chronicles. The Hebrew Bible describes this remarkable structure in various places, but most prominently in 1 Kings 6.16–28:

He built twenty cubits of the rear of the house with boards of cedar from the floor to the rafters, and he built this within as an inner sanctuary, as the most holy place. The house, that is, the nave in front of the inner sanctuary, was forty cubits long. The cedar within the house had carvings of gourds and open flowers; all was cedar, no stone was seen. The inner sanctuary he prepared in the innermost part of the house, to set there the ark of the covenant of the LORD. The interior of the inner sanctuary was twenty cubits long, twenty cubits wide, and twenty cubits high; he overlaid it with pure gold. He also overlaid the altar with cedar. Solomon overlaid the inside of the house with pure gold, then he drew chains of gold across, in front of the inner sanctuary, and overlaid it with gold. Next he overlaid the whole house with gold, in order that the whole house might be perfect; even the whole altar that belonged to the inner sanctuary he overlaid with gold.

In the inner sanctuary he made two cherubim of olive wood, each ten cubits high. Five cubits was the length of one wing of the cherub, and five cubits the length of the other wing of the cherub; it was ten cubits from the tip of one wing to the tip of the other. The other cherub also measured ten cubits; both cherubim had the same measure and the same form. The height of one cherub was ten cubits, and so was that of the other cherub. He put the cherubim in the innermost part of the house; the wings of the cherubim were spread out so that a wing of one was touching one wall, and a wing of the other cherub was touching the other wall; their other wings towards the centre of the house were touching wing to wing. He also overlaid the cherubim with gold.

When the First Temple was ultimately destroyed, the people of Israel went into exile. Exile and wandering are metaphors of punishment by God throughout the Bible, and then throughout the ancient and medieval eras. Remember what God asks Satan twice in the opening chapters of the book of Job: 'Where have you come from?' And Satan's response: 'From going to and fro on the earth, and from walking up and down on it' (1.7 and 2.2). Lack of stability was usually a sign of loss of favour in the sight of the Almighty, throughout the Hebrew Scriptures. But as God's people wandered, it was God who lived high on his holy hill, far away from the transience of human life.

And so, when medieval Christians came to believe that building great churches was something God would desire, they were taking their cues from Jewish tradition, the psalmists, all of Scripture: they were rebuilding the Temple, and rejoining God in a place that would not falter. Buildings had the ability to communicate divine power, and the sacred rites performed only within those sacred spaces were the most essential human activity on earth. The 'house of God' was taken literally to mean just that: God resided inside. They believed that God Almighty, the Triune, eternal Godhead, was uniquely present in church, and even more so in great churches. That is how Christians once understood God's presence.

God's presence in sacred space

The real delight in visiting any medieval church is worship. Moving beyond the roles of sightseer and tourist, the worshipper has the opportunity to participate in ancient rituals performed in solemn places made holy from centuries of use. To worship in a cathedral is to move in rhythm with an organism, for this is what such a place was created for. And what a privilege that is! But the experience is lost on those who walk through churches as if they are just like any other place.

On my first visit to the Abbey Church of Mont St-Michel, I arrived early for Mass (*Messe*), which was scheduled to begin at 12.15 p.m. Sitting in a sacred space originally created by thousands of men and women nearly 1,200 years earlier, I watched as members of the Jerusalem Community prepared for the service. This community of monks and nuns – also known by their full name, Monastic Fraternities of Jerusalem – was founded in 1975 with the intent of bringing the spirit of desert spirituality and Charles de Foucauld into the heart of cities and tourist locations; they took up residence in the abbey on Mont St-Michel less than a decade ago. Prior to that, decades of religious neglect had passed on the holy mountain.

A single nun sat on her haunches before an icon of Christ Pantocrator (an image that emphasizes Christ's role as 'Almighty'), placed on a tripod beside the altar. Trios of candles stood on the stone altar itself, flickering sweetly from the natural air currents caused by stone and glass and the warmth of the early afternoon sun quietly beaming in. Another nun, and then another, joined the first, as school children – one French group, another of German teenagers – began to troop in, making far too much noise. But within a few more minutes, the sanctuary naturally hushed as people began to take notice of what was happening in the chancel.

A few minutes later, a monk was standing in the transept and began to ring the massive abbey bell from a thickly corded pull rope. A flute began to play and that first, adoring nun was now joined by eight others, both nuns and monks, all sitting and waiting on their haunches with heads slightly bowed. One man, presumably a postulant of some sort, did the same, but in his civvies.

I sat in the choir surrounding the altar, a section of the church up front, slightly separated from the wooden chairs in rows in the nave. This was the pleasure of arriving early –

obtaining the best seats in the house. 'There are still a handful of places on Earth where it is inconceivable for a mobile phone to ring,' I thought to myself.

From the vantage point of the choir, contrasts in architecture were easily spotted. The chancel surrounding the high altar is more recent, pointed Gothic. It is often the case, in cathedrals all over Europe, that the choir has been redesigned in the Gothic style, over an earlier Romanesque crypt or nave. Canterbury Cathedral is another notable example of this. But nowhere in northern France did this contrast seem more important and clear than at the Abbey Church of Mont St-Michel.

> We can hardly imagine the impression which [Gothic] buildings must have made on those who had only known the heavy and grim structures of the Romanesque style. These older churches in their strength and power may have conveyed something of the 'Church Militant' that offered shelter against the onslaught of evil. The new cathedrals gave the faithful a glimpse of a different world. They would have heard in sermons and hymns of the Heavenly Jerusalem with its gates of pearl, its priceless jewels, its streets of pure gold and transparent glass (Revelation XXI). Now this vision had descended from heaven to earth.
>
> (E. H. Gombrich)[1]

The Romanesque-style chancel – surrounding the high altar – had collapsed, and was rebuilt in the second half of the fifteenth century. This was the era of the High Renaissance when St Peter's Basilica was under construction in Rome. Da Vinci, Raphael and Michelangelo were hard at work on refurbishing churches all over Italy, and Gothic principles had become more commonplace. In the Mont's remote chancel, thudded pillars were replaced by equally large ones (to hold up such a roof!), but designed to hide their strength in favour of verticality. Each pillar in the new (odd to say 'new' for the fifteenth century) chancel is diamond-shaped, made up of multiple mini/round-pillars, called colonnettes, fused together. These pillars create what is called an ambulatory or semicircle around the chancel, and small chapels stem from it like petals. Twelve narrow Gothic arches surrounded us in a half-moon in the ambulatory, while thicker, rounded, Roman arches sat within more simply rounded pillars surrounding the nave. Back around the altar, ten chancel pillars frame the twelve Gothic arches.

> What the roman could not express flowered into the gothic; what the masculine mind could not idealize in the warrior, it idealized in the woman; no architecture that ever grew on earth except the gothic, gave this effect of flinging its passion against the sky.
> (Henry Adams, *Mont Saint Michel and Chartres*)[2]

To sit in the choir of the Abbey Church is to worship in a diffused, thorough daylight. Light floods in behind and above the pointed arches – structures that Ken Follett calls 'doorways for giants' in his novel, *Pillars of the Earth*.[3] The sun above the sea was shining brightly on the first day that I was at Mass, warming the cold, acoustic stone. To look back from chancel and choir into the Romanesque nave is to go from light to shadow, points to rounds.

We sang Psalms 117 and 118 in French. I understood only as much as I remembered from my reciting of the psalms in English. 'Blessed is the one who comes in the name of the LORD.' But in those subtle ways that still bind many Catholics to the Tridentine Mass, I was fully able to sing together with the monks, nuns and the hundreds of others when we came to the Kyrie Eleison. *Kyrie Eleison. Christe Eleison. Kyrie Eleison. Christe Eleison* (Lord, have mercy. Christ, have mercy . . .).

> Beauty in architecture is conspicuous order – order shining out.
>
> (Eric Gill)[4]

Even dictators sometimes know better than to disregard the purpose of sacred spaces. It was Napoleon who said, '*Un athée serait mal a l'aise ici*' ('This is no place for an atheist') upon entering the Cathedral Notre-Dame de Chartres for the first time. That's about right. Inviting God into a space is perhaps the most basic, elemental form of spirituality that we can practise, and our medieval ancestors did it very well. It's no accident that you can sense it when you are in such a place – that simply means that you are attuned.

In a church context, this is often called the act of *consecration*, as when the priest consecrates the bread and wine in the service of Communion, or when a man or woman consecrates himself or herself to religious life, holy orders. Or when a congregation consecrates a new altar, or chalices, candles, vestments, for sacred purposes. To *consecrate* something is to set it apart for another purpose. That can be done with all sorts of things.

In a broader context, we choose whether or not to consecrate ourselves, our spaces, our relationships. '[L]ike living stones, let yourselves be built into a spiritual house, to be a holy priesthood, to offer spiritual sacrifices acceptable to God through Jesus Christ' (1 Peter 2.5). In other words, like any other holy space, allow yourselves to be consecrated.

The late medieval imagination was broadly sacramental, and places where the sacrament of Communion was practised were the most holy places on earth. Worship bound people together in a mystical way that is rarely appreciated today. The best explanation of this may come from Pope Benedict XVI's recent encyclical on love:

As Saint Paul says, 'Because there is one bread, we who are many are one body, for we all partake of the one bread' (1 Cor. 10.17). Union with Christ is also union with all those to whom he gives himself. I cannot possess Christ just for myself; I can belong to him only in union with all those who have become, or who will become, his own. Communion draws me out of myself towards him, and thus also towards unity with all Christians. We become 'one body,' completely joined in a single existence. Love of God and love of neighbor are now truly united: God incarnate draws us all to himself.[5]

Physical spaces were easily and completely filled with the divine. Emotion filled the minds and words of medieval men and women when they were in a magnificent church – in the presence of God in an especially sanctified space. In fact, many of the cathedrals were constructed on sites that had long-standing spiritual connotations. Archaeologists believe that the crypt beneath Chartres Cathedral originated centuries before Christ. It was perhaps once part of a temple to the goddess Isis, and revered as a place of feminine deity by the Druids when they inhabited the now-vanished woods of Chartres. One Renaissance commentator wrote about the timbered roof of the cathedral: 'The roof is commonly called the "forest," as much because of the prodigious multitude and quantity of wood as, perhaps, in commemoration of the fact that the forest or body of wood of the Druids formerly stood on the site.'[6] The only reminders of this legacy to the tourist today may be found in the New Age bookstore across from the south entrance of the cathedral.

Chartres is the earliest and most prominent example in western Europe of a conversion of what was pagan to Christ. It is often called the very first church of Gaul. The first Christians who came to Chartres witnessed the Isis temple but probably soon consecrated the space to the Virgin Mary, to whom Chartres Cathedral was also later dedicated. All of Chartres became the Blessed Virgin's place of honour, before the Gothic cathedral was ever built there.

> The endless upward reach of the great west front, the clear silvery tone of its surface, the way three or four magnificent features are made to occupy its serene expanse, its simplicity, majesty and dignity – these things crowd upon one's sense with a force that makes the act of vision for the moment almost all of life. There is an inexpressible harmony in the façade of Chartres.
>
> (Henry Adams)

The space of the first Gothic cathedrals were understood to be places of safety, communion and love. This was a moment in time during the Middle Ages when Christ's love, not Christ's anger, was the dominant image of relation to God. Images of God resembling a mysterious force of wind ravaging everyone in sight, as in a science fiction film, were foreign ideas to those who built the first Gothic cathedrals. You didn't find images of the Apocalypse or the Last Judgement in the Gothic structures at St-Denis or Chartres or Reims. God's presence was not felt through the anger of the Father, but through the compassion and creation of the Son. However, less than a century later the spirit of the times changed and the fear of God, like the Black Death that coincided with it, took over. The Gothic moment was brief – when the love of God the Son and the care of Mother Mary far surpassed images of a vengeful and fearsome God – and it is preserved for us in the great cathedrals.

Consecrating the world with beauty

Only in these most sacred of spaces was beauty conceived to be of such importance. The kitchens, bedrooms and work

21

studios of the Gothic era were not adorned, but the cathedrals were as nothing else. The earliest and most important of the Gothic architects, Abbot Suger of St-Denis, explains that he hurried to enlarge and adorn the upper choir of his abbey church because that was the place that saw the sacred re-enactment of the Eucharist that was central to faith: 'the continual and frequent Victim of our redemption'. There could be no more noble act of a Christian, he believed.

Beauty was a lively idea in the minds of religious people, in those days. According to the Qur'an, beauty is one of the ninety-nine names for God. And according to Pseudo-Dionysius, a medieval philosopher who inspired the Gothic worldview, beauty is the *only* name for God. Architects, builders and bishops – like Abbot Suger, who rolled all three of these jobs into one – believed that they simply knew what was beautiful when they saw it. And they took their cues from Scripture – in the descriptions of the First Temple or the New Jerusalem – for what God would recognize as beauty.

> Beauty will save the world.
> (Fyodor Dostoevsky, *The Idiot*)

Abbot Suger followed the traditions of the ancient Levite priests of Israel in his elaborate furbishing of St-Denis. The priests were instructed by the law of Moses to create sanctuaries fit for the presence of Yahweh. The Bible has Yahweh instructing, 'Make me a sanctuary, so that I may dwell among them. In accordance with all that I show you concerning the pattern of the tabernacle and of all its furniture, so you shall make it' (Exodus 25.8–9). Furnishings, tables, fabrics and hangings, a lamp-stand, curtain and altar are all described in detail, plus the oil for the lamps, the vestments for the priests, incense, basin, anointing oil, and the details for sacrifice. Suger adapted these guidelines in the twelfth century without any hint of the fearsome God that characterized the original Levites. Those original Hebrew high priests had pomegranates and bells attached to the lower hem of their robes: Yahweh said to Moses, 'Aaron shall wear it when he ministers, and its sound shall be heard when he goes into the holy place before the LORD, and when he comes out, so that he may not die' (Exodus 28.35). But you will struggle to find any symbols of God's wrath or judgement in St-Denis or Chartres cathedrals.

To consecrate a sacred space is not so much to allow God in, as it is to stand consciously in God's presence. It was the Gothic builders who perhaps understood better than any other Christians in history how the physical stuff of this world is our way of reaching out to the Divine. They used the sensuous to support faith. Eric Gill once wrote: 'Though the flesh lusteth against the spirit, they are only enemies of one another in the same way as the innkeeper is the enemy of the traveler and seeks to delay him.'7 The sacred space of a cathedral is supposed to be like a good innkeeper.

3

Making our places holy: sanctuary

—◆—

*Like living stones, let yourselves be built into a spiritual house
... Once you were not a people, but now you are God's
people.*

(1 Peter 2.5, 10)

Each person involved in building a cathedral – architects, masons, glass-workers, sculptors, manual labourers – shared specific ways of looking at the world. The work of constructing a great cathedral was much more than employment; it was divine work, done by skilled craftsmen. Each man or woman engaged in the work of building Chartres or Rouen or Caen cathedrals was first asked to make a general confession, and to offer certain vows of holy intentions for the work.

E. M. Forster in *A Room with a View* has his free-spirited character, Mr Emerson, confront a priest during a tour of Santa Croce in Florence. The priest is explaining that the great building was constructed in this sort of fervour of medieval faith, and Mr Emerson retorts, 'Built by faith, indeed! That simply means the workers weren't paid properly.' The German sceptic, Johann Herder, captured this same popular stereotype more than a century ago when he criticized, 'Europe was full of enslaved serfs, and the slavery which oppressed these people [building cathedrals] was all the harder, because it was a Christian slavery, regulated by political laws and blind tradition.'[1] In fact, cathedral-building was the most remarkable craftsmanship of its era, involving sophisticated geometry, materials and planning. Still, it is true that we should take the documents of the time with a grain of salt when, for instance, they declare with a rosy confidence that not a whisper was heard during work times, or that thousands of people engaged in carrying massive stones had completely 'lulled to sleep all vice' during those blessed years of construction. 'Their labour was their alms,' we read again and again in these documents of the period. 'Spiritual camps' is how one contemporary chronicler put it, to describe the places where workers worked and lived, with priests praying over them, and all was sounding a bit like the Peaceable Kingdom. Nevertheless, we do know that most of the labourers who worked on the great cathedrals had dignity in their work in ways that are absent from the labourers in most of today's largest factories. It has been said that no era ever comes to know its greatest people, and I believe this is true of the High Middle Ages in that we will never know the cathedral-builders. I envision them like shepherds in the fields or iconographers with their icons; they worked hard but they were expected to bring their reason and creativity to the task.

Economic, political and spiritual motives were all entwined in the building of cathedrals. Economically, the entire financial life of a city depended on pilgrimages being made to a cathedral. Politically, a cathedral brought prestige and centralized authority to a region. And spiritually, a cathedral brought the people together as a new expression of church. For example, on 10–11 June 1194, a terrible fire burned most of the famous medieval town of Chartres, including most of its cathedral. There was despondency throughout the town immediately afterwards, for what would happen to the livelihoods of the people of Chartres without their cathedral – their place of buying and selling goods, of trading with vendors from other regions, not to mention the draw that the cathedral was for pilgrims? It was an Italian cardinal, who had been sent by the pope, who persuaded the people to rebuild, and quickly. Politically, city officials were almost always religious officials, as well, and they knew that a strong Gaul was dependent upon a strong Chartres and that a strong Chartres was impossible without a vibrant cathedral. And then spiritually, after the Chartres fire, the people of France believed that perhaps the Virgin was angry with them, much like God's anger that resulted in the Great Flood. But that cardinal convinced them that the Virgin permitted the great fire because, in his words, 'She wanted a new and more beautiful church to be built in her honor.'[2] Most of the soaring Gothic structure that now stands in the place of the old one at Chartres was erected in just over a quarter century – which doesn't seem like a brief span of time, but was remarkable in its day.

* * *

The late Middle Ages were also the time of renaissance in human knowledge. It is no accident that the great Gothic cathedrals were built during the era that was also home to other efforts to synthesize all ideas into one. Thomas Aquinas was writing his magnificent and all-inclusive theological *Summa*, and Jacobus de Voragine was compiling his almost equally massive *Golden Legend*. The first was intended to collect and integrate all human knowledge toward God, and the second was the attempt to coalesce an encyclopaedic understanding of the lives of the saints up until that point. People were at a stage in their Christian faith – more than a millennium after the time of Christ – when they wanted to bring all knowledge and wisdom together into one place. The basic plan of a Gothic cathedral did this, as well, constructing all into one space.

> [W]hat we have said of the cathedral church of Paris has to be said of all the churches of medieval Christendom. Everything is of a piece in this logical, well-proportioned art, which originated in itself. To measure the toe is to measure the giant.
>
> (Victor Hugo, *Notre-Dame of Paris*)[3]

If you pay attention to the details while walking around a cathedral, you'll begin to take in a certain look and feel. This is how Gothic cathedrals impress one upon first experiencing them. There is what might be called a geometry to these places.

The proportions of a cathedral follow a certain unwritten geometry that was believed to have its origins in the Divine. Uniformity was the rule, and it followed numerical principles. The numbers three, five, seven, and sometimes nine and ten, were imitated, meaning that the same feature would be repeated seven times, or nine times, and so on. A certain logic results from this sort of design, which is why you might feel that you understand Gothic architecture easily upon first experiencing it.

Equilateral triangles and circles were used as ideal forms to shape as many features as possible. If you look at the Royal Portal (above the doorways of the primary entrance) to Chartres Cathedral, you will see images of Christ encircled by symbols of the four evangelists (central portal) and symbols of the ascension (left portal), each of which are designed within the parameters of a perfect triangle surrounded by circles. Look at these images and imagine drawing a triangle around the sculpture of Christ and circles around the evangelist symbols and angels to the left and right. Similar geometric designs are evident throughout the interior of the cathedral, in designs on the floor, the windows and elsewhere.

> [Human] senses delight in things duly proportioned
> as in something akin to them; for, the sense, too,
> is a kind of reason.
>
> (Thomas Aquinas)[4]

A cathedral was intended to supply nearly all of a person's needs. Somewhat like today's 150,000-square-foot retail spaces, designed to entice and keep you inside their walls for as long as possible, and even mega-churches on a similar plan, a cathedral was more than one thing in people's lives. A cathedral such as Chartres was a busy place where people of all backgrounds gathered to do business with each other. It was the centre of town.

> Merchants erected their stands in front of the canons' houses. The three squares just outside the cathedral were the scenes of the most lively activity. Fuel, vegetables, and meat were sold by the southern portal of the basilica, textiles near the northern one. At night strangers slept under the cathedral portals or in certain parts of the crypt. Masons, carpenters, and other craftsmen gathered in the church itself, waiting for an employer to hire them. Even the selling of food in the basilica was not considered improper if carried on in an orderly fashion. At one time the chapter had to forbid the wine merchants to sell their product in the nave of the church, but assigned part of the crypt for that purpose, thus enabling the merchants to avoid the imposts levied by the Count of Chartres on sales transacted outside. The many ordinances passed by the chapter to prevent the loud, lusty life of the market place from spilling over into the sanctuary only show how inseparable the two worlds were in reality.[5]

Pilgrims would often sleep on the nave stone floor of the cathedral. In fact, most architectural historians believe that the reason why the floor of the nave of Chartres Cathedral slopes nearly three feet from east to west (from the centre of the nave out to the primary entrance) is because of the convenience such construction would have provided for washing the floor of the messes left behind.

Artisans and workers placed themselves under the protection of the church and, depending on their form of work, under one of the saints of the church, as well. St Ambrose was the patron saint of beekeepers; St Francis of Assisi was the patron saint of merchants; St Jerome, librarians, and in the centuries after Chartres Cathedral was rebuilt, St Vincent Ferrer, a Dominican, became the patron saint of builders. A church viewed the people's lives and activity as essential to the greater organism. They functioned together like bees in a hive, dependent upon each other.

The active and contemplative sides of life were more firmly united in the lives of Christians than they are today. Both were of equal spiritual value, and the assumption was that one could not function properly without the other. This can be seen in sculpted images on the famous north porch of Chartres. These small figures can be difficult to make out when visiting these days, but they show everyday work coinciding with the Christian virtues. You will see depictions of young women doing household chores such as sewing and washing – symbolic of everyday activities that sustain our lives on earth – and then beside them are other images of young women occupied in spiritual reading and meditation. Nearby are the famous, small, bas-reliefs that show the Christian virtues (such as humility and perseverance) in allegorical form. The point seems to be clear – and it was not simply a theological point or one artist's unique vision – the cathedral is the place where all of life makes sense.

Architecture began like any other form of writing. It was first of all an alphabet. A stone was set upright and it was a letter, and each letter was a hieroglyph, and on each hieroglyph a group of ideas rested, like the capital on a column . . . Later on, they formed words. Stone was superimposed on stone, and those granite syllables were coupled together, the word tried out a few combinations . . . The Temple of Solomon, for instance, was not merely the binding of the sacred book, it was the sacred book itself. From each of its concentric ring-walls, the priests could read the word translated and made manifest to the eye . . . Thus the word was enclosed in the building.

(Victor Hugo, *Notre-Dame of Paris*)[6]

We may fault our medieval forebears for believing that the church building should be the centre of their universe. It's scarcely imaginable today. There was little beauty apart from order, and that order began inside the building. What happened inside was central to the meaning of life, more than what happened on the outside. Imagine this for a moment. Our medieval fathers and mothers believed that the literal centre of the universe was the altar on which the body of Christ is broken for us. Beyond the altar is the chancel, or sanctuary, and beyond the sanctuary is the nave where the people witness this miraculous act. Some naves are 300 feet long or longer, the size of a football field. The cathedral at Chartres was built to house 15,000 people, because the entire town was there once upon a time. Today, there are rarely more than fifty people present at a typical morning Mass.

The altar and the chancel should be the first things considered in a Catholic church. However plain the rest of the structure – however limited the means . . . these

31

should possess such a character as to point out at once their sacred destination.   (Augustus Welby Pugin)[7]

But why make these sanctuaries so beautiful, sometimes, extravagantly so? The beauty seems to contradict their usefulness.

At this point in our story, we should pause to consider that unique character, Abbot Suger of St-Denis, in greater detail. Suger (1081–1151) was born into a poor family and sent to the Abbey of St-Denis at the age of nine to become a monk. His life was fairly unremarkable until he was elected abbot of the same abbey in 1122. At that time, it was almost as though he was a child given the keys to the castle at too young an age. He lived extravagantly, arranging for valets and companies of attendants, counselling Kings Louis VI and VII of France, styling himself like a resplendent lord of the manor rather than a humble servant of God.

Then, enter Bernard of Clairvaux (1090–1153), the sometimes severe Cistercian monk and the most famous religious man of his day. Bernard wrote a public letter pointing out the excesses of Abbot Suger and others like him. Himself the son of high-born parents in Burgundy, Bernard nevertheless viewed the life of a monk to be in contrast to the world in a way that we might call 'puritanical' today. This strain has existed in the Church since the earliest days when survival was a Christian's ultimate concern. Tertullian (AD 155–222), for instance, ridiculed those in the early churches who were 'lighting useless candles at noonday', and argued that if you have the true light of Christ within you, you don't need candles as votives for additional illumination.[8]

For Bernard, spiritual beauty was distinct from worldly beauty. As one writer has put it,

St Bernard's contemporary eulogists assure us – and his modern biographers seem to agree – that he was simply blind to the visible world and its beauty. He is said to have spent a whole year in the novitiate of Citeaux without noticing whether the ceiling received its light from one window or from three; and we are told that he rode a whole day on the shores of Lake Geneva without casting a single glance upon the scenery.[9]

It was this Bernard who took any abbot to task who would presume to play the part of a high-born lord. But Abbot Suger listened to Bernard, and converted his behaviour, completely changing his personal habits – but not his attitude toward beauty when it serves God.

Suger refocused himself on reforming his monastery and, in fact, brought spiritual discipline as well as fiscal responsibility and growth to the place. He always saw his role as providential, and began to take on new projects – projects that surely disappointed Bernard of Clairvaux once again. Above all else, Suger's greatest work was the overseeing of the transition of the now-famous church of the Abbey of St-Denis from the late Romanesque style to the Gothic. There is some question as to whether or not Suger functioned as his own architect, but he certainly oversaw every detail of the work. Massively thick walls and columns and semicircular arches were turned into the new style with pointed arches, ribbed vaulting, and all of the adornments that we now easily associate with *Gothic*. He famously wanted St-Denis to be 'upward-leading'.

Sometimes Suger sounds extravagant. He wanted the world's most brilliant gems and brightest gold to adorn the walls of God's church. He was childlike in his enthusiasm, but also brilliant in his ability to defend his actions and opinions against the complaints of others. His writings are unique to the time period for their confessional and frank nature. Many scholars have, in fact, referred to him as the most valuable historian of his age. In one of his books, he explains how he added costly gems to the main altar in imitation of what had once been done to the Ark of the Covenant:

> Often we contemplate, out of sheer affection for the church our mother, these different ornaments both new and old . . . then I say, sighing deeply in my heart: *Every precious stone was thy covering, the sardius, the topaz, and the jasper, the chrysolite, and the onyx, and the beryl, the sapphire, and the carbuncle, and the emerald.* To those who know the properties of precious stones it becomes evident, to their utter astonishment, that none is absent from the number of these (with the only exception of the carbuncle), but that they abound most copiously.

And then, he explains some of the reasons why:

> The loveliness of the many-colored gems has called me away from external cares, and worthy meditation has induced me to reflect, transferring that which is material to that which is immaterial . . . then it seems to me that I see myself dwelling, as it were, in some strange region of the universe which neither exists entirely in the slime of the earth nor entirely in the purity of Heaven; and that, by the grace of God, I can be transported from this inferior to that higher world in an anagogical manner.[10]

It was common for the cathedral architects to refer back to the Hebrew Bible and the Temple of Solomon, the Ark of the Covenant, and the vessels that were known to adorn the altars of the First Jewish Temple. But Suger used these ideas to bolster his reasons for reserving the absolute best of the world for Christian worship. 'To me,' he wrote,

> one thing has always seemed preeminently fitting: that every costlier or costliest thing should serve, first and foremost, for the administration of the Holy Eucharist.

If golden pouring vessels, golden vials, golden little mortars, used to serve, by the word of God or the command of the Prophet, to collect the blood of goats or calves or the red heifer: how much more must golden vessels, precious stones . . . be laid out . . . for the reception of the blood of Christ![11]

I know that this world is a world of imagination and vision. I see every thing I paint in this world, but everybody does not see alike. To the eyes of a miser a guinea is more beautiful than the sun, and a bag worn with the use of money has more beautiful proportions than a vine filled with grapes. The tree which moves some to tears of joy is in the eyes of others only a green thing that stands in the way . . . As a man is, so he sees. As the eye is formed, such are its powers.

(William Blake)[12]

Not everyone agreed with the extravagance of Suger's remodelling project. In fact, many questions were raised that are similar to questions that come up today. Bernard of Clairvaux thought that Gothic principles were haughty, unnecessary, far too expensive, and he remained one of Suger's most severe critics. Bernard had, in fact, criticized what he thought were excesses in the reforming church architecture of his own Cistercian order, principles and adornments that were far less ambitious than were Suger's, before Suger had ever arrived on the scene. Bernard persisted for many years, continuing to write letter after letter to Abbot Suger, castigating him for squandering wealth on matters that should only seek purer, spiritual meaning.

But Suger of course felt differently. He viewed the jewel-encrusted religious objects as an antidote to vulgar culture and society, where the sacrifice of Christ was entirely forgotten or devalued. He is unapologetic about his views that churches should be adorned with the most beautiful objects on earth. At one point, Suger takes note, entirely without guile, of a 'merry but notable miracle which the Lord granted us' when two famous abbeys of Bernard of Clairvaux's own Cistercian order sold him some gems, 'when I . . . could not sufficiently provide myself with more'. The Cistercians who sold them to Suger surely knew the feelings of Bernard about such things, and were probably delighted to be paid handsomely for sapphires, rubies, emeralds and other gems that had been given to them as alms. They would have been thanking God for such a blessing, while Abbot Suger almost naively proclaims: 'We, however, freed from the worry of searching for gems, thanked God and gave four hundred pounds for the lot.'[13]

Suger adored his church – both the building itself and the people who would enjoy it – for the ways that the gems and splendours of the physical world were used to mirror the greater beauty of God and heaven. He said:

> The charm and beauty of this house of God, the splendor of the multicolor gems, lifts me beyond my everyday concerns, and in meditation I reflect on the diversity of the virtues, transposing what is material into what is immaterial. I feel as if I am living in some strange part of the universe which lies somewhere between the slime of earth and the purity of heaven. And so, by God's grace, I rise analogically beyond the inferior to the superior.[14]

In fact, he had an inscription made in copper-gilt letters on the newly gilded main doors into the great church that reads, in part,

> Marvel not at the gold and the expense but at the craftsmanship of the work.
> Bright is the noble work; but, being nobly bright, the work

Should brighten the minds, so that they may travel,
    through the true lights,
To the True Light where Christ is the true door.[15]

This seemingly simple abbot was a philosopher of aesthetics.

Much more recently, when St Patrick's Cathedral was built in New York City (foundation laid in 1853) it was a symbol of the triumph of an immigrant people – both Irish and Catholic – announcing themselves to their Protestant neighbours with the broad stroke of architectural grandeur. At the consecration of a new high altar in St Patrick's in 1942, Cardinal Spellman said, 'At its portals, the world seems left behind and every advancing step brings heaven nearer and deepens the soul's unity with Divinity.' Many New Yorkers will testify that to enter the building is a moving experience, an altogether different one than may be had in most other places around the city. But, I suspect, Cardinal Spellman's remarks are lost on most people who no longer share a world-view that comes close to that of the medieval cathedral-builders.

A holy place

The next time you stand inside a cathedral, look around at the walls and ceiling and imagine, as they once did, that you are glimpsing the entire created universe with Christ's altar at the centre. In the sanctuary, a word that literally means 'holy place', they created a place of safety and asylum for all who enter. This has been true of churches since the end of the Roman Empire, and it is essential to the spirit of a cathedral: it is *for the people*. The living stones (*lapides vivi*) of the verse from 1 Peter that heads this chapter were understood to be a holy house, or sanctuary, where the Church universal is undivided. In fact, the earliest under-standing of the meaning of *Church* is that it is all people, whether they know it or not. All human beings are one organism striving for a way to find their way home.

In our own day, these meanings of the word *sanctuary* have been renewed in tangible ways of support to the poor and oppressed. The New Sanctuary Movement is the name for a loose confederation of churches that are actively protesting the deportation policies of their federal governments by sheltering families that are, for whatever reasons, living in a country illegally. In the United States, the New Sanctuary Movement is active in at least thirty-seven cities, with families living within the church buildings themselves.[16] This gives an active, fresh meaning to the principles of *sanctuary* that began long ago. The churches of Abbot Suger and throughout the Gothic movement were places where Christians were in the presence of God and each other, made holy. The cathedrals were new ways to experience sanctuary and to experience the true nature of the universe itself.

A friend of mine once remarked that, as she walks forward to receive Communion each week, she doesn't usually reflect on her own sinfulness, or on Christ's sacrifice, so much as on the soft sounds of everyone's feet on the stone floor walking all around her. I didn't fully understand her comment until I began to spend time in the great old cathedrals. Our medieval ancestors knew and experienced our essential unity in ways that went unspoken and have been mostly lost ever since their time. Pope Benedict XVI recently put it this way in paragraph 48 of his encyclical, *Spe Salvi*: 'No one lives alone. No one sins alone. No one is saved alone. The lives of others continually spill over into mine.'[17] Cathedrals remind us of these things.

4

A place that is cool: stone

———•◆•———

In the Middle Ages, people believed that all the world was full of symbols, revelations, hidden secrets of the divine plan. Absolutely nothing was accidental. Each word of Scripture, even the seemingly inexplicable ones, was fully intended by God. Each star in the heavens had a meaning for humankind, and it was up to humans to decipher it. Without knowing some of those symbols and secrets, it's nearly impossible to experience a great cathedral in any detail. For most people today, walking around cathedrals is like reading an old book that assumes you know certain Latin phrases (because everyone used to learn basic Latin in elementary school) or allusions to the Bible (because nearly everyone knew their Authorized Version).

Just as a sculptor has a plan for how to begin chipping away at the block of stone, medieval Christians believed that God had all the creation in his mind before he began to form it. And the work of church architects and builders aimed to replicate divine plans and intentions. Their way of seeing the world was to attempt, at every turn, to see the divine plan for creation and then to recreate it in their work.

Making something permanent

The stability of cornerstones and other permanent fixtures in great churches were intended to be symbols of the Almighty. Those elements that were likely to have been used by the people who constructed the Tower of Babel – stone, buttresses, even glass – were revived, and medieval builders saw God smiling on their towering cathedrals, as places where God was at home with God's people.

They felt that the massive Romanesque buildings of an earlier time no longer communicated the purpose of the Christian life. The Romanesque style is reminiscent of an imagination that was bent on safeguarding its possessions and property, and crusading against infidels. Beginning in 1056, popes had begun telling the people to take up arms and retake the Holy Land for Christ. Many of the first Romanesque cathedrals were built in this era of fortified castles and invading armies. Their thick, stalwart constructions were designed to protect the inhabitants and to thwart those who were seen as threats to Christian security and life.

The church as fortress

Several hours and about 200 miles from Paris is the islet of Mont St-Michel, sitting on the boundary between Brittany and Normandy. It is one of those 'sacred isles' of mystical memory, inhabited over the centuries by the strange, bizarre and unusual. One of the best things about visiting Mont St-Michel is the approach. It is not the most remote of French monasteries – that honour would probably go to the Abbey of St Martin-du-Canigou in the Pyrenees, built on a precipice – but remoteness was clearly one of Mont St-Michel's original intentions. And you must see it from various places around the countryside in order to properly approach it. The approach to the abbey is full of mystery. Legends speak of pilgrims walking in the danger of penance and the excitement of faith between the mainland and the islet, half a mile out. My elderly friend, Jane, remembers visiting as a girl in the 1930s and the old mariner who rowed her family across in his boat. The walkway and road were built in more recent days.

Mont St-Michel is a tidal island, today. The water level will change as much as fifteen metres from low tide to high tide. Medieval pilgrims once referred to the abbey as 'St Michael in Peril of the Sea', because it was dangerous to walk the flats quickly at low tide. Pilgrims who still walk it today can become stuck in quicksand on the silt-covered flats. This danger is central to why they built an abbey in such a place as this. Danger was part of the equation of religious life and every-day life. Henry Adams said more than a century ago that it's faith that holds up the buttresses of the Gothic churches: without faith they'd make no sense. Similarly, the danger of life on Mont St-Michel was essential to understanding something about God. Faith was beautiful, mysterious and dangerous, something that modernism and secularism can-not fathom.

I have no idea what it must be like to live in a place such as Mont St-Michel. I am accustomed to pavements and nearly identical suburban houses. Shopping malls with restaurants and large retail establishments that are repeated from one town to the next. But in a place such as this, not only are the sand and gravel ancient with associations, but one stands in the shadow of the abbey church, which can only be described as an unearthly sculpture. It is not divine so much as it is completely foreign to this world. Where did it come from but the imagination of Christians long before me? Mont St-Michel seems almost like Loch Ness; it holds a monster that may or may not exist.

> He brought me, in visions of God, to the land of Israel, and set me down upon a very high mountain, on which was a structure like a city to the south.
>
> (Ezekiel 40.2)

Fortress and *palace* are two metaphors that help to explain the basic differences between Mont St-Michel and Chartres, and between the Romanesque and the Gothic ways of approaching God. The medieval stone structure of Mont St-Michel is a fortress – and also home to an abbey. This holy mountain represents the perennial desire of humanity to save itself by strengthening one's position against one's enemies, both temporal and spiritual. The Roman Empire receded from this part of the world in the middle of the fifth century, but still, Roman footprints can be seen in every corner of this part of the world, and religious wars and intrigue have filled the hearts of men and women who have lived in these locales for just as long.

The Mont was, like most religious places, involved in worldly politics and violence during the heart of the Middle Ages. For example, the monks and lords who ruled the abbey and isle in 1067, just after the Norman Conquest of England, threw their support in with William of Normandy in support of his right to the throne of England. As was common in those days, showing allegiance led to financial gain and privileges; Mont St-Michel was given property on the English side of the Channel, in Cornwall, and encouraged to start Norman abbeys there that would relate closely to their own.

Throughout the fifteenth century, during the Hundred Years' War, the British attacked the fortified abbey repeatedly, although never successfully. The deep fortification of the abbey led to its use as a prison for a time, in the years following the French Revolution of 1789. This resulted in no great loss to religious life on the Mont, as it had all but died away by that time anyway. The Protestant Reformation was felt keenly there, and there were almost no monks left in attendance at Mont St-Michel by the time the peasants overtook Paris and spread their revolution throughout late-eighteenth-century France. Touring the holy mountain today includes seeing the instruments of torture and incarceration that remain. It remained a notorious prison until 1863. In the 1940s, during World War II, the beaches and tall cliffs of Normandy all around Mont St-Michel were battered during the invasions of the Allies retaking France. The American headquarters in Normandy were in the nearby town of Avranches, just across the bay; but the Mont escaped damage during that time.

In both physical and spiritual terms, Mont St-Michel is a fortress. The Italian-born architect, William de Volpiano, who was hired by Richard II of Normandy to build the abbey church, dared to build it at the pinnacle of the Mont. This would seem like an odd choice, unless you were living in that time when church, state and power were intricately intertwined. It made perfect sense that the top of the Mont would be a church, and that the ramparts and battlements for military defence would be all around and below it. But this also meant that for stability's sake, multiple crypts and chapels and other supports would be carved into the side of the rock, beneath and around. Touring it today, you wouldn't know how tall the abbey actually is, or how high you have risen above sea level, as it stands on top of other buildings, but also because height is not what's on your mind.

Elements of this fortress of faith still remain. But between 1450 and 1520, the thick Romanesque sanctuary of the Abbey Church of Mont St-Michel was reconstructed as Gothic. The days of fortressing were passing, and the era of making palaces for God was beginning. To walk about in the abbey today is to experience stark differences between the two architectural styles. And to visit other Gothic places such as St Ouen or Canterbury Cathedral or Chartres Cathedral is to see how other churches represent a palace far more than a fortress.

The purpose of stone

If a photograph is worth a thousand words in depicting most aspects of life, then perhaps the right words are worth a thousand photographs of your friend's recent trip to see the great Gothic cathedrals. I have taken some marvellous photographs in cathedrals, but rarely if ever have I felt that they actually captured what is there to be experienced. Photographs often make the most beautiful saints depicted in stained-glass windows look absolutely lifeless. Photos of sculpted figures never seem to capture the vibrancy and spirit of the originals. So it is with the stones of the medieval cathedrals. The rough-cut slabs and blocks, which were fixed above the ancient crypts of spiritual sites so long ago, seem to breathe with the centuries of Christians who have walked and knelt upon them in ways that are never captured in picture postcards.

Imagine trying to describe a marvellous classical music concert to a friend after it ended. The feel of the room, the way that they tuned up beforehand, the look on the conductor's face, the sound of the violins or the oboes during a sumptuous passage. How could you either photograph it or describe it adequately? You cannot. Perhaps photographs do not capture the feel of a medieval cathedral because the cathedrals themselves were designed never to capture their subject. This is one of the great ironies of a place like Chartres or Canterbury or Wells or Reims: they were crafted as palaces to honour every detail that we might know of God from the Bible, tradition and the writings of the early church fathers and mothers – and they were believed to be places where God literally resided and came alive – and yet, their architects and truest believers never presumed to have spoken clearly or certainly about their Great Subject.

The central area of any Gothic church, the big space that holds the congregation, is called the nave. *Nave* derives from the Latin *navis*, which means ship. A nave is supposed to look like Noah's ark. In a large cathedral, the nave is designed to contain every human being within reach; it is supposed to be the place of salvation for all. I would surely have been struck, even from a distance away, by the sheer height of the nave. It's difficult to put oneself in the mindset of a previous imagination, but those were the days before human hands had built anything taller than the Gothic cathedral, and it was no accident that the tallest buildings were the religious ones. I wouldn't have asked my companions, 'Why is it so tall?' Instead, I probably would have fallen on my knees, recognizing that I was in a place made holy by God's presence. That's what human hands created – a place with the power to instil those sorts of feelings in human beings. My spiritual perspective would have been very different, back then, from what it usually is, today.

It was the American novelist and essayist, Annie Dillard, who wrote twenty-five years ago in *Teaching a Stone to Talk*:

On the whole, I do not find Christians, outside of the catacombs, sufficiently sensible of conditions. Does anyone have the foggiest idea what sort of power we so blithely invoke? Or, as I suspect, does no one believe a word of it? The churches are children playing on the floor with their chemistry sets, mixing up a batch of TNT to kill a Sunday morning. It is madness to wear ladies' straw hats and velvet hats to church; we should all be wearing crash helmets. Ushers should issue life preservers and signal flares; they should lash us to our pews. For the sleeping god may wake someday and take offence, or the waking god may draw us out to where we can never return.[1]

That's how I would have understood things, had I lived in Chartres, France 600 years ago.

Like the nave, each aspect of the cathedral was symbolic of God's expansive presence, as well as the presence of God's people, and it was stone that formed the foundation.

*   *   *

It is an interesting task to walk around a great cathedral today and to ponder the original meanings of the stone gathered there. Beneath Chartres Cathedral is a crypt – layers of over-lapping piety of rocks and mortar – that is more ancient than Canterbury Cathedral, and nearly as large as St Peter's Basilica. The crypt itself is nearly 1,500 years old. A fire destroyed everything above ground in 1194, and all but the crypt was gone. Chartres had pilgrims even then, before any-thing Gothic was built on that holy site. It was a shrine to the Virgin before it became the most famous such shrine of the Gothic era. After the fire, it is thought that the crypt must have functioned as the church itself during the early years of rebuilding. Reconstruction would have focused first on the central piers and the choir. The piers were necessary supports, and the choir and sanctuary were the quickest way for a church to become a church once again. Then, services would have been held in the reconstructed choir as the nave and transepts were also being rebuilt.

Jean Gimpel, a historian of technology, has estimated that so much stone was quarried in northern France from the eleventh to fourteenth centuries that it would dwarf even what was gathered in Egypt during the era of the Pyramids.[2] The limestone of Chartres Cathedral was quarried almost entirely from an area about seven kilometres to the south and east of Chartres known as Bercheres-les-Pierres, or Bercheres the Rocks. Even today, this place holds some attraction for pilgrims, as it is difficult to imagine a place on earth where such stones might have come from. In fact, some of the most beautiful photographs of the cathedral have been taken from across grassy fields, en route to Bercheres-les-Pierres.

> Listen to me, you that pursue righteousness,
>   you that seek the LORD.
> Look to that rock from which you were hewn,
>   and to the quarry from which you were dug.
>   (Isaiah 51.1)

Back in the early thirteenth century, these rocks were quarried and carted with great procession into the city. I find myself trying to imagine not the men at work in the quarries, or with the carts entering the city, but the masons, whose job it would have been to mount those massive limestones. The quality of the stone of Chartres is unmatched, and its colour and tone have mellowed to a beautiful pinkish-yellow over the centuries that reminds me of the rosy beauty of the stone of Mount Subasio that adorns the Basilica of San Francesco in Assisi, another great Gothic construction.

The first 'word' that Francis of Assisi heard from God, as he knelt in the abandoned and dilapidated San Damiano Church near Assisi was, 'Go and repair my house, which, as you can see, is falling down.' He was searching for meaning in his life, and searching for God at that moment, and those were the first words he heard in his soul in answer to his many questions. Simple-minded in his early vocation, Francis did not then imagine fixing big problems within the Church universal. Instead, he understood himself as one who could repair churches, one by one, with his hands. He simply began gathering stones, and begging the people of Assisi to give him stones. This all happened sometime around the year 1208, in the middle of that twenty-five-year period during which the nave of Chartres Cathedral was being built in the Gothic style. Francis' father was a wealthy cloth merchant who often travelled across Italy to France and then returned with news from abroad. We do not know for certain, but it is intriguing to think that Francis of Assisi might have been inspired by both God and the quarrying going on in the Loire River valley.

The masons who worked on the late medieval cathedrals tended to move from town to town, big job to big job, from year to year, as many of them were highly sought after. They were usually members of large guilds of like-type craftsmen, and they periodically entered into negotiations about salary and work conditions, similar to today's trade unions.

We know that the architects and guild-workers who were engaged in building great churches would also sometimes influence the building of parish churches, nearby, on smaller scales. Hundreds of towns throughout France were inspired by what was happening in Chartres. And news spread rapidly to other lands, as well. As one historian of medieval parish churches in England describes it:

> a large monastic or cathedral church in process of erection was a source of inspiration to the less skilled builders of a parish church in the same neighbourhood; methods of construction would be gleaned and details copied, and as a result the advances being made in Gothic development by the great building masters, to whom experiment was the breath of life, were in due course reflected to a limited extent in the architecture of the parish church.[3]

Stonework was the most fundamental art of the new cathedral movement. But all things considered, these still were not glamorous jobs; in fact, no physical work was glamorous in the Middle Ages. Since the Greek philosophers had established a difference between liberal arts and mechanical arts, the stone mason, like the fresco painter, was considered a manual labourer even though he was a great artist. All mechanical artisans were seen as manual labourers, distinct from the landed or intellectual classes who would hire labourers to work for them. But this also means that the great frescoes which adorn the walls of a basilica or cathedral were painted by men no less respected than the great masons who laid the foundation for that same basilica.

The majority of houses in Europe at that time were timbered, and to build with stone was something especially reserved for palaces, public buildings and churches. The stones of a cathedral such as Chartres symbolize the holy martyrs upon whom the Church universal is built. So do the columns that connect the ancient stones with the high ceilings above; medieval builders saw a natural connection between these aspects of their constructions. Theirs was holy material. And ultimately, the great stones – usually the oldest part of any cathedral – were symbols of Jesus Christ. 'For no one can lay any foundation other than the one that has been laid; that foundation is Jesus Christ,' as St Paul says in 1 Corinthians 3.11.

> A frail moan from the martyred saints there set
> Mid others of the erection
> Against the breeze, seemed sighings of regret
> At the ancient faith's rejection
> Under the sure, unhasting, steady stress
> Of Reason's movement, making meaning-less
> The coded creeds of old-time godliness.
> (Thomas Hardy, 'A Cathedral Façade at Midnight')

Stone took on fresh dimensions in the Gothic cathedrals. Stones were asked to accomplish and symbolize new things. Stoneworkers and architects aimed to use this most enduring element and make it do new things that communicate spiritual truths once enclosed only in books. Upon looking at great Gothic structures for the first time, observers often notice how surprisingly tall they are. It is natural to wonder how it was possible for these towers to hold up, since they are made almost entirely of stone and glass, two extremely dense and heavy elements. One guidebook remarks about the famous Gothic-style Cleveland Tower at Princeton University's Graduate College, 'It seems to revoke the law of gravity; stone rises as if lighter than air.'[4] Another commentator a century ago wrote of Chartres, 'The stones, it seems, have become intelligent, and matter is here spiritualized.'[5]

Stone was also used to create more statuary than ever before. This is another way that the stone cathedral became the book without words – the way of communicating the story of Christianity better than any form of writing had done. The art of the Middle Ages was concerned with tiny details in addition to enormous structures. The smallest of details might escape our notice as we visit the French cathedrals, but it is in these details that the stories are told. For example, on the north porch at Chartres, there are little figures under the feet of more recognizable ones. They are charming but important. Everyday tourists stand and take their photographs in the afternoon sunshine, but each has a specific meaning. A donkey, for instance, holds up the biblical figure of Balaam; in Numbers 22, it is this donkey that sees an angel of the Lord who has come to speak with Balaam, even before Balaam sees it. The angel tells Balaam that if it were not for the donkey's perception, he would have killed Balaam. In another spot on that porch, the Queen of Sheba is supported by one of her servants – surely one of the select ones who helped her transport gold and precious stones from the East to meet King Solomon and honour his God (1 Kings 10).

Other stone figures and their supports are more theologically nuanced – as, for instance, the one also on the north porch at Chartres of the burning bush of Moses resting beneath the feet of the Virgin Mary. Medieval theologians often compared the bush that was on fire before Moses' eyes, burning but not consumed, to the virginity of Mary which was unchanged after the conception and birth of

Jesus. Similarly important at Chartres are the images in the windows – those enormous windows that would have made the construction untenable were it not for the use of buttresses. The windows tell stories just as the stones do. In one window, for instance, the Old Testament prophets are seen to hold up the four evangelists of the New Testament: Matthew (Isaiah), Mark (Daniel), Luke (Jeremiah) and John (Ezekiel), showing the Christian belief that the life of Jesus was the fulfilment of the prophecies in the Hebrew Bible.

The stones of Gothic churches are often smaller, and occasionally quite irregular, as compared to the great stones used in Greek and Romanesque buildings. A pre-Gothic building, whether church or not, was simply intended to be sturdy, to perform its tasks and for as long as possible. The strength of the Gothic structure, in contrast to those that had come before it, was not derived from its enormity but from its synchronicity. Walk around the floor of the nave at Chartres, all around the area that is home to the famous labyrinth, and ponder the slabs of stone. Some are square, but very few; others are rectangles; and some have sharp pointing edges that still fit in with the pieces all around them. These ancient stones are what we kneel on during Mass, and I can't help but wonder at the people who have kneeled in the same place, for eight centuries, before me.

> Arise, my love, my fair one, and come away. O my dove, in the clefts of the rock, in the covert of the cliff, let me see your face, let me hear your voice; for your voice is sweet, and your face is lovely.
>
> (Song of Solomon 2.13–14)

The mass of stones that make a Gothic cathedral is the saints who have built the Church universal. The medieval builders and the people knew as much. Harking back to the Temple of Solomon in 1 Kings, the stones, in all of their uses and configurations, were a place suitable for God, and a heavenly city of and for God's people. In the Song of Solomon, God invites the Church into his clefts and coverts, a theme that is picked up again in one of the most beautiful passages from the Gospels:

> In my Father's house there are many dwelling-places. If it were not so, would I have told you that I go to prepare a place for you?   (John 14.2)

*   *   *

Medieval people were realists, not nominalists. This means that they believed created things were never isolated in meaning or use, but instead participated in 'forms' of divine origin. In other words, when we use a word such as *stone* to describe what is underfoot, or what the altar is made of, *stone* has more meaning than simply what is walked upon or what the paten and chalice sit upon. There is a 'form' of stone that ultimately participates in heavenly meaning. This is critical for understanding what the medieval mind saw while walking around or worshipping in a cathedral. All they had for their best belief and faith was the realism of the created things, to know God and his world as best as they were able. The names we have for God have profound meaning, and with a spirit-filled imagination, we can begin to know him inside a cathedral.

The medieval philosopher, Pseudo-Dionysius, wrote in one of his classic works, *Divine Names*:

> On no account therefore is it true to say that we know God, not indeed in His nature (for that is unknowable, and is beyond any reason and understanding), but by the order of all things that He has established, and which bears certain images and likenesses of His divine para-

digms, we ascend step by step, so far as we can follow the way, to the Transcendent, by negating and transcending everything and by seeking the cause of all. Therefore God is known in all, and apart from all.[6]

*   *   *

Notre-dame de Chartres! A world to explore, as if one explored the entire Middle Ages.   (Walter Pater)

As you enter any of the great cathedrals of Europe on a warm spring or summer day, a rush of cool air greets you. If you were prone to mystical fancy, you might think that God was greeting you as spirit. Or, if you are more practically minded, it is almost as if they have the air conditioning turned up high – until you realize that it's the effect of the stones that you are feeling. I remember, during a summer in the Philippines, how I and my friends loved to go to the cinema in Manila on brutally hot afternoons because it was only there that it was air-conditioned. I can imagine people feeling similarly about Gothic cathedrals not too long ago in Europe.

During one quiet moment in Chartres Cathedral, I slipped off my shoes to feel the stones underfoot. Medieval people used their senses to taste, see, listen, smell and touch the Divine. They expected to experience God in some small measures, directly. I don't mean that they experienced God sensually in credulous ways; there have always been methods for testing truth (there were friars who doubted St Francis of Assisi's stigmata wounds during his own lifetime). The point is: the medieval imagination never doubted an experience of God simply on the grounds that it was sensual. And that morning, I used my toes to trace the outline of the stones under my chair and imagined who might have stood or walked or knelt in that place centuries ago. Just as I was beginning to feel sheepish about doing something so foolish, I looked across the aisle at a woman doing just the same thing who had at that moment looked up and taken solace that she was not alone, either.

5

Open your eyes and see: light

―――•◆•―――

Before the printed word, the churches were the Bibles of the poor, and the Church was my first book.

(John McGahern)[1]

There seems to be a vague feeling of inexplicable spirituality that comes to many people, even the most unbelieving, when standing in a great church. It's not uncommon for the tourist to feel a bit overwhelmed sitting or walking about in a place like Canterbury or Chartres Cathedrals, St Peter's Basilica or Westminster Abbey. Just as looking at the sun setting over water can make almost anyone feel like Wordsworth or Pan, it doesn't take a mystic to admire the Creator upon entering a great church. These are places where God is easily felt and, as we've already begun to explore, that's according to plan.

Light *robes* things in its hidden splendors.

(Matt Torpey)[2]

Lux and lumen mean something very different today from what they meant in the thirteenth century. Today, to those who can speak the language of photometry, lux and lumen are part of an international system of units for measuring the perceived intensity of light. These terms are used to measure light's visible luminosity. But in the thirteenth century, they meant something quite different, as terms used only by theologians. Derived from the same Latin word (meaning 'light') *lux* was the term used for the eternal light, the one used by God in creation, and *lumen* was the refraction of that eternal light throughout the world. For the Gothic architects, *lumen* reflected *lux* in and through the features of a cathedral. They saw an intrinsic connection between natural light and inspiration: both were divine, and they had a necessary relationship.

The principle aim of the Gothic architect was to make masses of stone appear simultaneously lighter and vaster, and to create a soaring upwardness in the reconstruction of Romanesque churches. This was accomplished by flooding natural light into the space as well as refracting it through colourful stained-glass windows. Church buildings were intended to tell a story, not simply house a congregation – and the story was enhanced in the Gothic style by the ways in which it depicted the Christian community in prayer. That's the whole idea of the pointed arch versus the rounded ones. If the Romanesque style was to emphasize the massive foundation and cornerstone of the Almighty, the Gothic was intended to put the Christian soul back into the building, bursting out of it, showing the fervour of faith in pointed arches, ribbed vaulting, pointed windows and towering ceilings. Everything was designed to draw the eye towards the heavens.

All of this was enhanced by flooding light into the building. Windows grew much wider, walls were thinned, and ceilings soared taller and taller. Gravity was transformed in the Gothic cathedral. This is the essence of what happened in places like Durham, Canterbury, Reims, St-Denis, Chartres: churches became, for the first time, more than functional. They became intelligent, ideological and contemplative. Windows grew not just large but enormous, especially in the cathedrals of France, where both clear and rose windows became a way of radiating natural light into the space of God. In fact, there were even moments, early on, when the new cathedrals were so tall, thin and full of glass that they were about to fall in or over – which is why flying buttresses came into being (but more on that later).

We live in a time when the world is lit up every night. We flip the lights on when we enter a room after the sun has gone down. There's nothing that we can't do at night indoors that we do during the day. Well, of course, it wasn't always so. Before the incandescent light bulb was invented, there were coal, beeswax, olive oil, fish and whale oil lamps, and as early as the fifteenth century such lamps were hung at night in the windows of houses on the city streets of London and Paris and elsewhere. But before those days, during the High Middle Ages, people lived in candle-shadows in the evenings. Conversations happened at night that would have been more uncomfortable during the day. Ghosts and spirits wandered at night. And darkness made room for criminals, disturbances, sexuality, and plenty of other secrets. 'What a difference there was between the imposing cathedrals with their polychromatic stained glass reflecting the glory of God, and the often dark houses crowded around them,' wrote one French scholar.[3] To approach an illuminated church after dark was to see a new sort of heaven, a place where the grandeur of God would be at home.

> . . . the light divine so penetrates
> The universe, according to its merit,
> That naught can be an obstacle against it.
> (Dante, *Paradiso*, canto xxxi)

If Gothic was the beginning of intellectual and contemplative cathedral construction, where did these ideas originate? It was Plato's student, Plotinus (*c.* AD 204–270), who first got the medieval mind churning with ideas of how natural light and divine light relate to each other, and how human inspiration relates to both of them.

Plato's thought was part of the intellectual atmosphere of the first-century world into which Jesus was born. The cities of the Roman Empire were full of discussions of Platonic ideas: the contemplation of truth, the difference between 'forms' and their physical appearances on earth, and the immortality of the soul. It was into this atmosphere that Jesus lived, preached, died and was resurrected. Into the Platonic worldview, St Paul said those words that sound so simple, and which we repeat so easily, but were an important new way of imagining what it means to adore God: 'To live is Christ.'

It's important to realize, of course, that Plato and Aristotle were not Christians. They lived and taught centuries before Christ. For that matter, so did Noah, Moses and prophets such as Jeremiah and Isaiah, but those biblical characters lived and taught in service to God, in ways that were faithful to God's working in the ancient world. Some of the theologians of the Middle Ages saw the pagan perspective of Plato and concluded that his writings were unsuited for Christian inspiration. An additional reason why Bernard of Clairvaux, whom we've already met, disapproved of Gothic architecture was because he disapproved of its intellectual inspiration. It was Bernard who once advised a student to turn away from the Greek philosophers and toward the Scriptures, by saying: 'I grieve to think of that subtle intelligence of yours and your erudite accomplishments being worked out in vain and futile studies . . . What will you answer at that dread tribunal [at the end of time, when Christ returns] for having received your soul in vain?'[4]

But for some other Christian thinkers throughout the Middle Ages, such as St Augustine, Plotinus' teachings were a non-Christian bridge from worldly secularity to true Christian orthodoxy. Plotinus spoke of the One, the ultimate uncreated source of all being, expanding on Plato's notion of the form of the Good. A Christian theist could adopt this language easily, and Augustine (although he regretted not finding many Christian-specific doctrines in the writings) credited the *Enneads* of Plotinus with first showing him that spiritual beings can exist, the depths of the human soul, and the reality of the ultimate, Immutable Light.[5]

This Ultimate Light is called by various names in Plotinus' writings, including The Unity, First, One and Cause. '[I]t cannot be a being,' he wrote, 'for a being has what we may call the shape of its reality but The Unity is without shape.' And like the God of Christian faith, the One cannot ultimately be described in its essence, but we can approach and hint at it:

> [W]hen we speak of this First as Cause we are affirm-
> ing something happening not to it but to us . . .
> strictly we should put neither a This nor a That to it; we
> hover, as it were, about it, seeking the statement of an
> experience of our own, sometimes nearing this Reality,
> sometimes baffled by the enigma in which it dwells.[6]

Plotinus also outlined how a human soul progresses to the One, or God. And this is what is most important for considering the perspective of Gothic builders on how best to utilize natural light. How does a human being come to know or see or experience God? Is it at all possible? In what measure is it possible? And how, exactly? For Plotinus – and then for many medieval theologians in varying related ways – there were three stages, each building on the one before it. First, a person may use reason to see the universe all around, the creatures and things, and thereby come to some basic wisdom from these experiences. Second, one may then see with a sort of interior vision the soul that is within oneself. By doing this with patient and subtle understanding, a person can begin to see the divine side of the world, although seriously veiled. And third, one may intuit, again through the soul that emanates from the Divine, and come to know God.

Our intuition, the Gothic architects concluded, is aided by seeing. And what aids our vision more than natural light? The natural light required to see in the world emanates from the one, divine Light. Lovers of Scripture, including ancient and medieval Christians, easily applied the 'light' of the physical universe to the interior 'light' of divine and personal revelation:

> The people who walked in darkness
> have seen a great light;
> those who lived in a land of deep darkness –
> on them light has shined.
>
> (Isaiah 9.2)

Images of eagles abound in Gothic cathedrals because the eagle is a symbol of the ascension of Christ and the soaring Gospel of John. Medieval men and women believed that the eagle was the only created thing that could look directly into the sun. An eagle loves the light and is drawn by it. St John's Gospel – the most poetic, mystical and theological of the four – takes us like an eagle on its wings to heaven.

Three centuries after Plotinus came another thinker who more than any other inspired this late medieval theology of light. The light that emanated from God the Father to God the Son became housed and demonstrated in the construction of Chartres – and an anonymous medieval theologian inspired what happened there. No one knows his precise identity, which is why his odd name begins with 'Pseudo'. He lived during the late fifth and early sixth centuries. He fused the Neoplatonic thought of Plotinus with the beliefs of an orthodox Christianity, and gave inspiration to the architects of the great cathedrals.

This is how he got his name. In the book of Acts, chapter 17, there is mention of a historical figure, a man from Athens (home of the philosophers), who was converted to the fresh Christian faith by St Paul. The text simply reads,

When they heard [as a result of Paul's teaching] of the resurrection of the dead, some scoffed; but others said, 'We will hear you again about this.' At that point Paul left them. But some of them joined him and became believers, including Dionysius the Areopagite and a woman named Damaris, and others with them.

(verses 32–34)

That's the first and last that we hear of the Athenian philosopher *Dionysius* in the Bible. Later, tradition has it that this same Dionysius travelled to northern France after his conversion, after leaving St Paul's company, and that he preached, converting many, and was eventually martyred there.

Nearly five centuries later, when the medieval (not the biblical) *Pseudo-Dionysius* (he was likely an anonymous monk whose writings were distributed narrowly at first) began to write, showing his erudition and subtlety of insight, he claimed to know biblical figures – to, figuratively, 'speak with angels'. This was not an uncommon way of expressing the idea that he believed his words were inspired by God. Since Pseudo-Dionysius claimed to 'know' characters in the Bible, making him seem to be a contemporary of them, many people of the Middle Ages thought that they had discovered ancient first-century texts in his book, *Mystical Theology*. Combine this with his love for the thought of Plato and Plotinus, and we come to see that his contemporaries identified the man as Dionysius – the actual biblical character. For all they knew, the writings that they were reading were much older than they actually were, and were perhaps written concurrently with holy Scripture. This is how our medieval philosopher has come down to us with the name of Pseudo-Dionysius.

Pseudo-Dionysius began to be quoted by the early sixth century, and by the year AD 600 Pope Gregory the Great was turning frequently to him. All of this seems mostly harmless, except for the added fact that the most influential Gothic cathedral happened to be the Abbey Church of St-Denis, north of Paris. St Denis, for whom the abbey was named, was martyred in the middle of the third century and was likely to have been a disciple, two generations removed, of the Dionysius who was converted under St Paul in Athens according to the biblical book of Acts. However, by the middle of the Middle Ages, the two men – Dionysius and Denis – were confused together; and as the Abbey Church of St-Denis claimed to have the relics of St Denis, they also believed that their connection to Dionysius was sincere. They were then among the leaders of those who came mistakenly to believe that the anonymous writings of the Pseudo-Dionysius were actually the writings of the original Dionysius. In other words, the 'Pseudo' did not exist in those days – not until another philosopher, Peter Abelard, began to set things straight in the year 1121. But Abelard was ahead of his time, and was not listened to on this point; instead, he quietly moved on, leaving the secure Abbey of St-Denis in order to become a hermit nearby. This was only twenty years before Abbot Suger relocated the valuable relics of St Denis to a position of utmost authority, under the high altar of the new Gothic palace he was creating. And thus, the important historical accident comes full circle: Abbot Suger believed that Pseudo-Dionysius' writings were inspired, perhaps even as much as Scripture.

For Pseudo-Dionysius, all things emanate from God. Symbols, images and revelations are essential and vital and also, all that we have. His theological outlook became typical of the late Middle Ages in that it focused intently on the manifestations of God in the things and images of the created world – but also in that, ultimately, we cannot know or see anything of God in essence. Pseudo-Dionysius meditated on the invisible world of God, and reflected on how it permeated our own universe. He divided the world into three hierarchies, that of Theos, the celestial bodies, and the ecclesiastical, otherwise known as God's people. All of this was done as a way of praising a God whom we cannot ultimately know with our intellects.

On the south porch of Chartres Cathedral, you may see nine choirs of angels, creatures of light, that were first categorized in the writings of Pseudo-Dionysius and carved there in order of their rank in heaven. From most important to least: seraphim (allowed to stand before God, according to Isaiah 6), cherubim, thrones, dominations, virtues, powers, protectors of nations, archangels and angels. He wrote that the greater the order of angel, the more brilliant the light that they exude. By this measure, seraphim would be, like God, impossible for the human eye to see because of their brilliance.

Pseudo-Dionysius saw God as the supreme Light and the incarnate Christ as the earthly image of that Light. He turned often to the fourth Gospel:

In him was life, and the life was the light of all people. The light shines in the darkness, and the darkness did not overcome it . . . The true light, which enlightens everyone, was coming into the world.

(John 1.4–5, 9)

And then, there's this passage from 1 John:

This is the message we have heard from him and proclaim to you, that God is light and in him there is no darkness at all. If we say that we have fellowship with him while we are walking in darkness, we lie and do not do what is true; but if we walk in the light as he himself is in the light, we have fellowship with one another, and the blood of Jesus his Son cleanses us from all sin. (1 John 1.5–7)

Pseudo-Dionysius taught that the universe is a potential and real irradiation of goodness and beauty, stemming ultimately from the light of God. He writes in his book, *The Divine Names*, that God's name is Beauty, and God imparts his beauty to all things 'according to their nature', by 'flashing upon them'. Historian Georges Duby summarizes the doctrine of Pseudo-Dionysius in this beautiful way:

> One idea: God is light. Every creature stems from that initial, uncreated, creative light. Every creature receives and transmits the divine illumination according to its capacity, that is, according to its rank in the scale of beings, according to the level at which God's intentions situated it hierarchically. The universe, born of an irradiance, was a downward spilling burst of illuminosity, and the light emanating from the primal Being established every created being in its immutable place. But it united all beings, linking them with love, irrigating the entire world, establishing order and coherence within it. And because every object reflected light to a greater or lesser degree, the initial radiance brought forth from the depths of the shadow, by means of a continuous chain of reflections, a contrary movement, a movement of reflection back toward the source of its effulgence. In this way the luminous act of creation brought about of itself a gradual ascension leading backward, step by step, to the invisible and ineffable Being from which all proceeds ... God was absolute light, existing more or less veiled within each creature, depending on how refractory that creature was to his illumination; but every creature in its own way unveiled it, for before anyone willing to observe it lovingly, each creature released the share of light it contained within it. This concept held the key to the new art – an art of

light, clarity, and dazzling radiance. This was the art of France, and Suger's abbey church was its prototype.[7]

When Abbot Suger oversaw the rebuilding of the west façade of the Abbey Church of St-Denis, he was not only influenced by Pseudo-Dionysius, but he also articulated the principle of *anagogicus mos*, or the 'upward leading method'. Low and thick Romanesque designs were trapped in darkness in ways that Suger wanted to overcome with light. Suger's desire was to get as close as possible through church architecture to the one true light of God. To literally let God in. Flooding light into the sanctuary is precisely what the Gothic cathedral does.

Light became the primary symbol of humankind's path to heaven. An inscription on the west façade, written by Abbot Suger, explains this theory in terms more poetic than theological:

> Noble is the work, but the work which shines here so nobly should lighten the hearts so that, through true lights they can reach the one true light, where Christ is the true door . . . the dull spirit rises up through the material to the truth, and although he was cast down before, he arises new when he has seen this light.[8]

This was the primary purpose of redesigning any cathedral during the Gothic moment of the twelfth and thirteenth centuries: to let the light in.

> [L]ight is a divided thing upon earth, shining in this house and that, and yet remains one.
> (Plotinus, *The Enneads*)[9]

As I sat on a quiet, warm afternoon in the nave of Chartres Cathedral, I thought about the teachings of Pseudo-Dionysius, that the eternal Light is reflected and refracted in brilliant spaces and divine inspiration may follow. That's the purpose of the light, of course: inspiration. But it is also a real participation in the eternal Light. To the medieval man or woman worshipping in that same place, the light shining down is a thin but real vector of the Light of Christ himself. It is a mystical gift.

Julian of Norwich once said that the soul is at all times experiencing itself intimately wrapped up in God, whether we are conscious of it or not. Our souls, as the centre of where we communicate with God, may be clouded and not actually *see* the light most of the time; but imagine what is possible when we *are* conscious and the senses of the body meet the reality of the soul!

The physical qualities of a Gothic cathedral, so weighted with meaning over the centuries, all work together to shine the light. Pseudo-Dionysius wrote:

> Every creature, visible or invisible, is a light brought in to being by the Father of the lights . . . This stone or that piece of wood is a light to me . . . As I perceive such . . . things in this stone they become lights to me, that is to say, they enlighten me.[10]

To pray in a cathedral is to receive the Light, and my spirit was flooded in ways that I knew were not really about reason.

6

Learning to live with the light off: darkness

———◆———

There are those who rebel against the light,
who are not acquainted with its ways,
and do not stay in its paths.

(Job 24.13)

Since the book of Job was written, we've come to understand in sometimes subtle and sometimes not-so-subtle ways that light is good and darkness is bad. Monsters, evildoers and anyone living outside of accepted norms of society are said to love the darkness, to wait for us like thieves in the night, and to shrink away from the light, as they cannot stand it. Storytellers will speak of men (they are always men!) with *dark* hearts or spirits, and of virtuous maidens with golden locks of hair and glorious, luminous qualities that affect all around them, sometimes even to draw those dark men out of the shadows. In this imaginary world, when night has fallen on a city, bad things are said to happen. Our stories are full of bandits and maniacs who roam the moors and haunt outlying areas from their roosts in nearly abandoned, shadowed castles. Even beautiful things on earth have been said to combine darkness with evil. The serpent in the Garden of Eden was beautiful. The dark angels, like sirens, are beautiful. Optimism, in contrast, shines with morning glory.

A genre of novels known as 'Gothic fiction' arose in the late eighteenth and early nineteenth centuries, dedicated to

67

this sort of imaginary world. Begun with Horace Walpole's fascinating *The Castle of Otranto* (1764), these stories inspired the modern horror genre. The name Gothic was applied to these novels primarily because their plots were usually played out in Gothic-style buildings such as abandoned monasteries and ruined castles, but also because the monsters and ghosts and terror-producing villains (who were sometimes monks, nuns or priests) had all shrunk far away from the light. The creators of these fictions clearly didn't know one important aspect of the imagination that created Gothic cathedrals: darkness is often good for you.

The brightness of the sun was the image that Dante chose for Francis of Assisi, while images such as 'the dark side of the moon' or 'the madwoman in the attic' represent the foreboding. It seems that darkness has always been a popularized metaphor for the absence of goodness and the loss of hope. These perspectives naturally influenced the white European's perspective of dark skin colour. Novelist Joseph Conrad (1857–1924) typified racist attitudes toward Africa with his novel, *The Heart of Darkness*. Dark skin colour was equated with being less than human. Religions have done no better. Religions of all kinds since time began, from the Egyptian through Christianity and Islam, have praised the ways that light shines through darkness, as a primary symbol of salvation for the lost. We speak of being illumined or flooded with light, when we come to some fresh understanding of God, or indeed, everyday other things. Remember even the description of what happened at the transfiguration of Christ; the story is told in all of the Gospels except in John's:

> Jesus took with him Peter and John and James, and went up on the mountain to pray. And while he was praying, the appearance of his face changed, and his clothes became dazzling white. Suddenly they saw two men,

Moses and Elijah, talking to him. They appeared in glory and were speaking of his departure, which he was about to accomplish at Jerusalem. Now Peter and his companions were weighed down with sleep; but since they had stayed awake, they saw his glory and the two men who stood with him.   (Luke 9.28–32)

Dazzling, white, glory.

But then see what happened immediately afterwards, as the dazzling white that describes the original scene is suddenly gone in a cloud of darkness:

[A] cloud came and overshadowed them; and they were terrified as they entered the cloud. Then from the cloud came a voice that said, 'This is my Son, my Chosen; listen to him!' When the voice had spoken, Jesus was found alone. And they kept silent and in those days told no one any of the things they had seen.
                    (Luke 9.34–36)

If we listen to this account closely, there is a side of faith and spirituality that relies on darkness, rather than light, for illumination. We see the same in Gothic cathedrals.

In the High Middle Ages, the darkest time of year became the month for the celebration of Christmas. Scholars have argued that Jesus was most likely born sometime between March and September (easier to explain the presence of shepherds in the fields), but the name *Advent* was given to the darkest month in the northern hemisphere: December. The winter solstice marks when light begins to enter the world more and more, towards the end of Advent, but it is also the darkest moment of the year, remembered since ancient days by pagan celebrations of fire. This is when medieval Christians decided to remember the moment that the incarnate Christ came.

Deity above all essences, all knowledge, and goodness, guide of all Christians to divine wisdom, direct our path to the highest mountain of your mystical knowledge . . . [Your] unchanging mysteries are veiled in the dazzling obscurity of a hidden silence, outshining brilliance with the intensity of their darkness, adding the impalpable and invisible beauty of glory that surpasses everything else to our blind minds.

(Pseudo-Dionysius, *Mystical Theology*)[1]

According to Pseudo-Dionysius, the divine light only makes sense in as much as it reflects a divine darkness. Like appreciating the use of light in a Turner painting, you cannot really do it without the corresponding darkness. Pseudo-Dionysius is what is called an apophatic theologian, one who believes that God is ineffable and must ultimately be spoken of only in terms of what he is not. Dazzling becomes linked with obscurity and silence, and brilliance becomes not a metaphor for light but for darkness.

During the ancient and medieval periods, theologians often argued that heavenly bodies of light such as the sun and stars and moon are somehow essentially dark – in the way that a faraway star may be seen to twinkle – even though we perceive them to be luminous. These heavenly bodies were believed to participate in the Divine, who is also essentially Darkness. Plotinus even wrote that the soul comes to inhabit the body through darkness, and he called it *illumination*:

The huge illumination of the Supreme pouring outwards comes at last to the extreme bourne of its light and dwindles to darkness; this darkness, lying there beneath, the Soul sees and by seeing brings to shape; since it must go forth, it will generate a place for itself; at once body exists.[2]

As the theologians grasped these ideas in the High Middle Ages, they marked a deepening of the spiritual understanding of light and darkness – one that fell away from the Christian vocabulary and experience in more recent centuries.

> Were all my loud, evil days
> Calm and unhaunted as is thy dark Tent,
> Whose peace but by some Angels wing or voice
>   Is seldom rent;
>   Then I in Heaven all the long year
>   Would keep, and never wander here.
>
>   But living where the Sun
> Doth all things wake, and where all mix and tyre
> Themselves and others, I consent and run
>   To ev'ry myre,
>   And by this worlds ill-guiding light,
>   Erre more then I can do by night.
>
>   There is in God (some say)
> A deep, but dazzling darkness; As men here
> Say it is late and dusky, because they
>   See not all clear;
>   O for that night! Where I in him
>   Might live invisible and dim.
>   (Henry Vaughan, 'The Night', lines 37–54)

Many of the architects and builders of the Gothic cathedrals knew these experiences of darkness firsthand, and many of them knew the experience of contemplation, when the senses are of no use. There are dark places within a cathedral and they are not always simply those spots where light will not reach. They are intended. Dark places have their symbolism just as do the more frequent, lighted ones. It was the aim of the Gothic architect to redesign churches making the rounded arches pointed, the low ceilings vaulted, and the dark sanctuaries flooded with light from new and enormous windows. However, some of the most profound spaces are those where darkness is still the rule.

Two of the most beautifully dark places in Chartres Cathedral are the side chapels dedicated to relics and images of the Virgin. These were the sorts of sacred spaces that even the enthusiast for the Gothic style understood were better left unlit.

A side chapel is, by definition, a small place of worship located off the aisle of a church. They are common throughout cathedrals everywhere. They were not created by Gothic architects, but have been around since the first churches with naves were erected. A chapel, after all, is what the most basic church in the countryside is: a house for an altar – which means that Eucharistic worship may take place there – with enough room for a few worshippers. It was in the great churches that chapels became *side* chapels, from the aisles off the nave. (An aisleless nave would have no space or place for them.)

The two chapels in Chartres that I am referring to are both on the north side of the building, and one of them represents the most famous relic of the Virgin in existence: the Virgin's Veil, as it is called there, today, also known as the Sacred Tunic, as it was most often called during the Middle Ages. The other is known as the chapel for the Virgin of the Pillar, an image that is popular particularly in Spain. When fire destroyed the old cathedral in June 1194, the primary reason why the people despaired was because they believed that the Virgin had caused it to happen because of her displeasure with the state of the world and of France. To the medieval imagination, the Queen of Heaven was fully capable of destruction that might seem whimsical to us. It was an Italian cardinal who was visiting Chartres on a mission from the pope in 1194 who convinced the people of

Chartres that the Blessed Virgin was not unkind to them or unhappy with them. On the contrary, he said, the Virgin had allowed the fire to happen because she wanted an even greater cathedral. After this speech, delivered to cheers from the people of the town, men and women emptied their pockets and gave much of what they had, as well as their time and strength, to rebuild Chartres greater than had ever been seen before. That Sacred Tunic, or Virgin's Veil, was brought up from the crypt below in the days following the fire, and shown to the people with great effect, demonstrating that the most important gem of the church had not been destroyed by the natural disaster.

The Gothic reconstruction of Chartres is intended to honour the Virgin Mary. Chartres is her palace. Medieval Christians believed that she, too, had a knowledge of God that was both light and dark. She knew the glory and luminosity of the divine touch, but she also knew – earlier than anyone else – of the darkness that is a deeper way of coming to know God.

> Here as everywhere else throughout the Church, one feels the Virgin's presence, with no other thought than her majesty and grace . . . She wielded the last and highest power on earth and in hell. In the glow and beauty of her nature, the light of her Son's infinite love shone as the sunlight through the glass, turning the Last Judgment itself into the highest proof of her divine and supreme authority. The rudest ruffian of the middle-ages, when he looked at this Last Judgment, laughed; for what was the Last Judgment to her! . . . Her chief joy was to pardon; her eternal instinct was to love; her deepest passion was pity!
>
> (Henry Adams, *Mont Saint Michel and Chartres*)[3]

This spirituality of darkness deepened throughout the centuries after Pseudo-Dionysius, as his teachings profoundly affected others, most notably, the reforming Carmelites of the sixteenth century, Teresa of Avila and John of the Cross. It is John of the Cross who has become the most articulate spokesperson for the ways in which a Christian is to love and seek the darkness. Not all the time, of course, but darkness can lead to a deeper understanding of a life in Christ. John speaks of the 'dark night of the soul', which has become almost a cliché, today, used by psychoanalysts and film script-writers as if it is a universal experience. Of course, it is not. The 'dark night of the soul' (which began as the title of a long poem by John of the Cross, plus his commentary upon it) represents those times when a person of profound faith enters into a dark, or spare, arid and thirsty time period in relationship with God. The result can feel like doubt and loss of faith, but is rather to be understood that God has put that person in the dark for a time. There is illumination in darkness, just as there is plenty to learn when one's divine understanding and relationship seems to be flooded with light.

According to John of the Cross, a person of deep faith may, and perhaps should, actually seek the teaching of darkness. The first stanza of his poem begins,

> On a dark night,
> Kindled in love with yearnings – oh, happy chance! –
> I went forth without being observed,
> My house being now at rest.

This is an intentional journey to reduce the ability of the senses to divert one's attention. We may put ourselves in this place, or God may put us there, as John explains in his commentary, 'drawing forth the soul from the life of sense into that of the spirit – that is, from meditation to contemplation – wherein it no longer has any power to work or to reason with its faculties concerning the things of God.' Then, as the third stanza so beautifully puts it,

In the happy night,
In secret, when none saw me,
Nor I beheld aught,
    Without light or guide, save that which burned in
    my heart.[4]

On my recent visit to Chartres, I prayed in the chapel dedicated to the Virgin's Veil. The placard describes the garment
as the one worn by the Virgin Mary at the time of the birth
of Christ in Bethlehem. It was given to Chartres by Emperor
Charles the Bald in 876, and – as was common in those
days – used almost as a weapon in battles against their enemies.
(Another book should be written about the influence of
Charles the Bald. The grandson of Charlemagne, he was
the one who invited the philosopher John Scotus Eriugena
to teach in his imperial court; and it was Charles who gave
other valuable relics to the cathedrals throughout France.)
One account has it that the veil was displayed in a battle in
911, like a monstrance holding the Holy Eucharist held
above one's head, and Norman armies fled in fear. Similar
stories abound throughout the next two centuries.

Despite the heroics, this is a relic of the humblest origins,
and seems almost out of place in a palace like Chartres. Ancient
and medieval Christians connected Mary with 'the poor of
the Lord', an image from the Hebrew Bible. Mary's life is full
of examples of how she lived far from wealth and privilege.
Her presence throughout a great cathedral doesn't change
those facts. The concept of the poor of the Lord is mentioned
by the prophets Zephaniah (3.12) and Isaiah (66.2) and
refers to a spiritual remnant in Israel, the humbled who will
one day be exalted. Jesus was probably remembering these
poor of the Lord when he preached the Beatitudes in his
Sermon on the Mount. Jesus went into the synagogue on the
Sabbath in Nazareth and read these words from the prophet
Isaiah: 'The Spirit of the Lord is upon me, because he has

anointed me to bring good news to the poor' (Luke 4.18). Earlier, in the scene where Mary, Joseph and young Jesus flee Herod's soldiers, the Holy Family resembles today's refugees, wandering without home and in search of a place of safety.

The cathedral is supposed to be that place of safety. And Mary's graciousness extends to all people who come to her in prayer. It is precisely these sorts of reminders that the builders have intended to surround in so dark and thoughtful a place as this chapel. As you sit or kneel there, look up at the windows above your head. There you will see more images of Mary, particularly the one known as Notre-Dame de la Belle Verrière, and all of them show the face of a woman who knew joy as well as sorrow. Mary was the first disciple of her Son, and she knew earlier than anyone else what his fate would be. The great window shows this side of her – she is seated on a throne looking forward, wearing blue gowns, with Jesus upon her lap. Like any good mother, she beamed with pride, was often joyful, but also grieved over what would come.

The prophet Jeremiah foreshadows the role of Mary as one who cries tears for us and is ready to help us before the Divine. The prophet's words foreshadow Luke's words depicting the women who followed Jesus during his time of passion.

> Thus says the LORD of hosts: Consider, and call for the mourning-women to come; send for the skilled women to come; let them quickly raise a dirge over us, so that our eyes may run down with tears, and our eyelids flow with water. (Jeremiah 9.17–18)

This is one of the many reasons why Christians have come to Mary as mother ever since gospel times.

I observed a woman, that day in the side chapel, who appeared to be from south India. She was clad in a red sari, with a scarf wrapped around the top of her head in reverence, and kneeling before the Virgin of the Veil on the bare floor. I watched her for several minutes. I found myself staring and then thought to myself, 'Is anyone noticing that I'm staring?' Of course not. Everyone was doing what they were doing, moving from chapel to chapel, seeing the sights, and then, some of them, making their petitions nearby, like the red-sari woman who was kneeling on the floor. 'I could do that for about one minute,' I thought to myself, 'before my knees would begin to scream out in pain.' I moved to one side, thinking that perhaps I was getting in the way of pilgrims who had clearly come with the express intention of visiting this particular chapel of the cathedral. So then I waited, seated comfortably nearby. The red-sari woman remained there, motionless, for thirty-five more minutes in the near darkness. Then she left and walked back outside into the light. All of this reminded me of John of the Cross' beautiful explanation of how darkness ultimately prefigures the light to come.

When Solomon had completed the building of the Temple, God came down in darkness and filled the Temple so that the children of Israel couldn't see. Then Solomon said: 'The Lord hath promised that He will dwell in darkness' (1 Kings 8.12). The Lord also appeared in darkness to Moses on the Mount, where God was concealed. Whenever God communicated Himself intimately, He appeared in darkness, as may be seen in Job, where scripture says that God spoke with him from the darkness of the air (Job 38.1). All of these mentions of darkness signify the obscurity of the faith when Divinity is concealed, when It communicates Itself to the soul. All of this will be ended when, as St Paul says, that which is in part shall be ended, which is this darkness of faith, and that which is perfect shall come, which is the Divine light. Consider the army of

Gideon; it is said that all the soldiers had lamps in their hands, but they still couldn't see because they had the lamps concealed in the darkness of pitchers. Only when the pitchers were broken, was the light seen (Judges 8.16). So does faith, which is foreshadowed by those pitchers, contain within itself Divine light, which, when it's ended and broken, at the ending and breaking of this mortal life, will allow the glory and light of the Divinity, which was contained within it, to appear.[5]

7

Don't take yourself too seriously: gargoyles

———◆———

There is no need that we should all be self-conscious prigs. There is no need to rule out gaiety or bodily enjoyment or even buffoonery, and we should learn to appreciate what we may call God's own coarse humour.

(Eric Gill)[1]

Eric Gill's profoundly incarnational understanding of God and the world – ideas that are often repeated and praised today in books of spirituality – still hasn't really rubbed off enough on us. The incarnation of God in Christ made the divine sensuous. This is a primary theme of the Gothic cathedral, experienced in the art of the stained glass, the stone underfoot, the dizzying height, the statuary on the porches and the portals, and the images all over the choir screens. But our vision of God still tends to be more refined and reserved, rather than passionate and active. We haven't yet digested the profoundly incarnational way that the High Middle Ages understood God. But look around any Gothic cathedral and you cannot help but sense it. The Gothic moment in history was all about experiencing Jesus as creator, sustainer, lover.

Later in the paragraph quoted above, Eric Gill continues: 'Rocky mountains, grassy downs, rats, germs, and dung, all are things singing to us of Him.' It might just be that the twisted, most unusual, aspects of created life are sometimes our best viewfinders for discovering spiritual things.

Cathedrals show how harmony and joy make less sense on their own, as they do when combined with a little bit of darkness and uncertainty. John Ruskin once ranked 'the characteristic or moral elements' of what best defined the Gothic sensibility, listing them in the following order of importance:

1 Savageness
2 Changefulness
3 Naturalism
4 Grotesqueness
5 Rigidity
6 Redundance

Savageness – which he also called, Rudeness – led the list.[2] The incarnate God can be unsettling, both in himself and in what he means for our understanding of ourselves.

Classical art was of a more idealized kind, a more refined taste, hinting at spiritual secrets rather than portraying what is most real to the human body and experience. But in the century that saw the birth of the Gothic style, medieval writers were rediscovering images of nature as symbols of the divine. Adam of St Victor (d. 1146) held a nut in the palm of his hand and declared it to be an image of Jesus Christ. With profound natural imagination, he saw metaphors in the fleshy green part (Christ's humanity), the hard outer shell (the cross), and the kernel which we eat (Christ's divinity). A century later, painters such as Cimabue and Giotto were giving renewed attention to the human figure in their frescoes in the hill-towns of Umbria. Mystics, painters and sculptors were returning people's attention to the link between the Divine and what they saw in nature.

The iconography of Chartres Cathedral was a renewed kind of humanism on the forefront of its time. On the famous north and south porches of the great cathedrals, Christ and Mary and the saints were depicted in designs of great trees of life, but with a realism that was unlike the earlier, idealized periods. Concern was paid to the folding of a garment, the angle of one nose versus another, and the fingers and toes of all sorts of creatures human and angelic. One expert offers a vivid example:

> The [figure of] Peter shows definite study of nature: he is more temperamental, with fuller lips; he is a human being more oriented toward life, with a more abrupt forehead, a peculiar, egotistically pointed and protruding nose, and a fleshy cranium . . . The hair, voluminous and heavy, lies in small, thick, spiraling curls. A deeply incised groove, not visible in the pictures, divides the beard. The sheer volume of the head is frightening and the vigorous jutting forward of the chin from the neck contributes to this impression.[3]

The human form, made sacred by the incarnation of Christ, was given its due by the early sculptors of Chartres and other French cathedrals. This was a period of early sacred humanism.

> The Incarnation may be said to have for Its object the drawing of men from misery to happiness. Being the act of God It is the greatest of all rhetorical acts and therefore the greatest of all works of art.   (Eric Gill)[4]

The Jesus of the Gospels, the Son of Man from Nazareth, the child of Mary, was renewed in the sculpture of the transepts and porches of Chartres, and in the Gothic sculpture of many other late medieval cathedrals. We see Christ as his followers had experienced him, doing things that the Gospels speak of him doing, and in ways that make human sense to us. Today we call these sculpted figures saints and, in so doing, we dismiss them without much thought. Such a perspective would have been impossible to the late medieval imagination. For them, saints were holy but never other-worldly, because the 'other world' was constantly touching this one. As one historian has explained, 'The history of the world is the history of the saints, and the geography of the world is that of their hermitages, their miraculous springs, their tombs and their pilgrimages.'[5] In the quarter century when they were originally carved, it would have been understood that saints are those to whom I am intimately related. To pray to a saint was to be physically as well as spiritually together with him or her. They appear common before the eye in the typical Gothic sculpture or painting, rather than idealized, and that's intentional.

But we also are reminded of figures and situations that are part of the Christian narrative but are also less pleasant and less common. There are gospel stories of the disfiguring brought on by disease, oppression of peoples, demon-possession, not to mention the Apocalypse, anticipating the end of the world as we know it, and other frightening things. The Gothic imagination includes all of these things, too. On the south porch of Chartres we see many sculptures of the damned going to hell, seemingly good-looking people, women and men, standing with devils behind them and holding them fast. Above these are sculptures depicting the resurrection of the dead; they emerge from their caskets and rise to the world above to join the faithful who are already there. These are all biblical images brought to life.

But in addition, there are extra-biblical images throughout Chartres and other cathedrals that represent the human fear of the unknown. Like us, the Gothic sculptors responded to what scares humankind with humour and self-deprecation. The weird shapes and disfigured, somewhat-human images peering out from the rooftops of the cathedrals are subtle ways of poking fun at ourselves when we are the most serious. I'm talking about gargoyles and grotesques.

These unusual figures had little precedent before the ancient era. The first known grotesque images come from the walls of caves in the Roman Empire during the time just before Christ. These are also often called chimera, and include mythical and fantastic creatures.

The medieval Christian imagination turned this simple technique into an art form of sculpture on the sides of their cathedrals. These figures took on a meaning similar to a comedian who has the ability to make us laugh because he performs caricatures of ourselves. At St Saviour's Church in Dinan, Brittany, for instance, you'll see a snake eating an owl, an idiot standing between two griffins, and then also the head of a bishop on an animal's body, and a man's face with a finger in his mouth. Nothing stands out more startlingly to me as I tour a medieval cathedral than these disfigured, partially human and frightening figures peering out from above or grimacing from underfoot of some great saint.

A gargoyle is 'a grotesque spout, representing some animal or human figure, projecting from the gutter of a building (especially in Gothic architecture)', according to the *Oxford English Dictionary*. But this sort of definition is too narrow for our use. Gargoyles are a special design of gutters, designed to move rainwater away from a building, but Gothic architecture is full of grotesque images that appear in various places around the outside of a cathedral – not necessarily as gutters.

Some people say that grotesques became extravagant in the twelfth century because the population was superstitious and illiterate, and so the Church created images that would both shock and strangely appeal. Some theologians say that grotesque images represented the gospel, which casts out all evil. Scribes were known to pen grotesque figures in the margins of religious manuscripts as they read – not from feelings of piety, but rather, a sort of playfulness, or willingness to engage with what was evil in the midst of what is supposed to be most holy. Others say that the growing recognition of naturalism in art gave way to a similar realism in depicting the reverse side of what is good and holy. Foliage and flower carvings appeared on capitals and columns, and both animal and human forms became realistic. The figures depicted on Gothic porches are almost animated. The best of them, as at Chartres, date from the late twelfth century and, by then, their creators were beginning to rediscover the human form. Beards flow; noses differ from one another; and gowns drape, showing the form underneath. These realistic, saintly figures make the monstrous figures lurching above, and in the recesses, all the more disturbing. All of these explanations are probably correct.

But gargoyles and grotesques are also simply playful. Marginal monsters live on the edges of medieval religious manuscripts, and also on the edges of cathedrals. The contrast between the solemnity of what's practised inside the building, and the playful, sometimes grotesque, monsters that look down on those who enter, make the whole thing seem a bit sinister and provocative. They are intended to be ironic, but also to bring smiles to the faces of those who see them. Imagine pondering the most profound of spiritual truths in the text of a classic document, and then grinning ear-to-ear at the image of an ass chewing on a bishop's clothes, off in the corner. That was precisely the artist's intention! It was Dante who assigned one of the circles of hell to the most gloomy among us:

> Bogged there they say: 'Sullen were we – we took
> No joy of the pleasant air, no joy of the good
> Sun; our hearts smouldered with a sulky smoke;
> Sullen we lie here now in the black mud.'[6]

The actual images of Gothic gargoyles and grotesques arose most often in the imaginations of those who designed or built them. They are not usually Greek or Roman or reproductions of any specific legendary creatures; they are monstrous and real all at the same time. They are whimsical creations. They are the outgrowth of what lies in the human soul and psyche – our ways of dealing with the fact that God expects us to be perfect, but it almost always seems impossible to be so!

> God will judge those outside. 'Drive out the wicked person from among you.'
>
> (1 Corinthians 5.13)

Monasteries and cathedrals were intended to create spiritual spaces, setting them apart from what was on the 'outside', or 'beyond the boundaries'. Medieval minds were big on fear of the beyond and unknown. Their ability to imagine monsters went unparalleled by other peoples and societies. By the early fifth century, in fact, even St Augustine of Hippo was so convinced of the existence of monstrous creatures and peoples that he listed and defended them in his famous book, *The City of God*. He lists creatures/people 'with their heels where their toes should be', and others 'but a cubit high, called pygmies by the Greeks', still others who were 'neckless, with the face of a man in their breasts', and many other types including those that he called Sciopodes – commonly found in the margin illustrations of medieval manuscripts – and so named 'because they sleep under the shade of their own foot'.[7] Augustine concludes that, if these all exist – and he certainly seems to accept that this is likely – then they, too, are descended from Adam and have souls just like the rest of us.

Grotesques are an acceptance of the idea that the world is full of relationships between creatures, as well as between the created and the uncreated, and these relationships are concealed, their ultimate meanings and connections being hidden from us. It is all contained in God, whose great idea began and sustains everything.

> From now on, the cathedral itself, formerly so dogmatic
> an edifice . . . escaped from the priest and came under
> the sway of the artist. The artist built to his own fancy.
> Farewell mystery, myth and law. Now it was fantasy
> and caprice. Provided the priest had his basilica and
> his altar, he had no further say . . . The book of archi-
> tecture . . . belonged to the imagination, to poetry and
> to the people.   (Victor Hugo, *Notre-Dame of Paris*)[8]

Grotesque creations were full of caprice and fancy, and they
spoke to the medieval imagination about what lurked
among humanity just as the altar spoke to medieval people
about the real presence of Christ in their midst. The fanci-
ful and sometimes foolish was intended to keep the real
and serious in its proper perspective. As one scholar has play-
fully inquired: 'What do they all mean, those lascivious apes,
autophagic dragons, pot-bellied heads, harp-playing asses,
arse-kissing priests and somersaulting jongleurs that pro-
trude at the ends of medieval buildings, sculptures and
illuminated manuscripts?'[9] The answer? These images on
the edges give the proper amount of levity and perspective
to a people's intention to become holy and to be with that
which is holy.

They are not intended to make any intellectual or spiri-
tual point other than this: don't take yourself too seriously.
The great Emile Male explains those on the outside of
Rouen Cathedral this way, better than I ever could:

> They swarm with monsters, but monsters ingeniously
> and wittily conceived, as if the work of vigorous young
> sculptors, vying with and outdoing one another. A
> rearing centaur wearing a cowl and bearded like a
> prophet shows two horse's hoofs as forelegs, two
> human feet in boots behind. A doctor in the cap of the
> faculty . . . stud[ying] a test-tube, is a man to the waist
> only and then becomes a goose. A philosopher with a

pig's head meditates as he holds his snout, a young teacher of music, half man half cock, gives an organ lesson to a centaur . . . If ever works of art were innocent of ulterior meaning surely these are.[10]

Fear arises from the unknown, and often if it succeeds in prompting us to action, laughter is not far behind. A gargoyle's smile can be like a clown's, a little bit frightening while it prompts us to giggle. The medieval imagination poked fun at itself, at that grand synthesis of all things, which simultaneously held that God had all created things in perfect mind before they came into being. We can be scared at the unknown, but we can also laugh in its face.

8

Reaching to heaven:
flying buttresses

————◆◆◆————

Height or the vertical principle, emblematic of the Resurrec-
tion, is the very essence of Christian architecture.
                                     (Augustus Welby Pugin)[1]

As we have seen, the introduction of the Gothic style of architecture was also the flowering of a new kind of spirituality.
Historians will say that Gothic flourished because rival
cities throughout Europe competed with each other to create the new architecture just as they competed for commerce
and influence. The same cities that had prominent Greek and
Roman temples and statues in late antiquity became the places
where the new, pointed style took off. But it was much more
than that.

The time period of the first Gothic cathedrals was when
many aspects of late medieval spirituality really began. The
builders of early Gothic were embarking on a very real,
new sort of crusade. In contrast to the Crusades that were
underway to retake the Holy Land with armies, through
battle, sieges, pogroms and other horrible actions (advo-
cated in the preaching of none other than St Bernard of
Clairvaux), these new crusades were for building beautiful
and sumptuous churches. New spiritual spaces, made holy
by human hands joining in God's work, rather than fight-
ing to reclaim holy places from ages past. Thus began an era

89

of unprecedented creativity and an expansive vision of who God is, and who human beings are.

Christians did not invent the idea of sacred space, but in places like the chancel of Mont St-Michel or in Chartres Cathedral they literally took it to new heights. What differentiates the Gothic style is its insistence on maximizing sacred space through light and height. At Chartres, they created a pilgrimage church through technical achievement: greater length (422 feet) and height (116 feet) than had ever before been attempted; larger windows than ever before; a vaulted ceiling that shocked the pilgrim with the way that those windows rose so high above the upper capitals. The nave – that inner space intended to hold 15,000 pilgrims at once – became a place for the people, in contrast to castles and palaces of a secular kind to which the typical man or woman may never have approached. The Gothic cathedral was a special moment in history and a new expression of how to be church.

The conversion of warring crusades to cathedral 'crusades' was clear in the work of Abbot Suger of the Abbey Church of St-Denis; he initiated the first surge of Gothic sensibility after listening to stories that were told by returning knights and monks from the Crusades to the Holy Land. He once reflected on the adornment of his own church in contrast to the wonders of the ancient East with these words:

> I used to converse with travelers from Jerusalem and, to my great delight, to learn from those to whom the treasures of Constantinople and the ornaments of Hagia Sophia had been accessible, whether the things here could claim some value in comparison with those there. When they acknowledged that these here were the more important ones, it occurred to us that those marvels of which we had heard before might have been put away, as a matter of precaution . . . Thus it could

happen that the treasures which are visible here, deposited in safety, amount to more than those which had been visible there.[2]

It's what the people of the Gothic period thought that flying buttresses accomplished that matters, much more than any argument about their intrinsic qualities. How was the faith of the people in the late Middle Ages formed by the designs of their holy spaces, and how might it help today's post-Christian Christians to recover some of the same?

Let me tell you a short anecdote. I was walking in New York City the other day and passed two different people on the street that caught my attention. Each of them was accompanied by an animal. In the morning, I was walking along Sixth Avenue and passed by a middle-aged man strolling down the pavement – with a black cat sitting quietly and comfortably on his hat, atop his head. The cat just sat there, looking around, as if this was the most normal way to wander around town. And then early that evening, I was sitting in the window of a restaurant having dinner. Hundreds of people walked past my window during the hour I was sitting there, but the one who caught my eye was a young woman, apparently home from work and now out on the street, walking her young dog. She and the puppy did not simply walk past the window, as everyone else did; they halted, over and over again. They would take three or four steps and then she would stop, pulling gently on the leash, and the dog would stop half a second later.

The dog was learning basic commands, while the cat was learning to be a bit more acrobatic. It seemed to me over dinner, as I thought about the two experiences, that they were fresh examples of creativity and form. I cannot imagine why the man had his cat on his head or, for that matter, why the cat was so willing to go along with such a thing. While, on the other hand, I know perfectly well why the woman was walking haltingly, and why her puppy was paying close attention.

The last element of the cathedral that we will take a look at is the flying buttress. The spirituality of this unique aspect of Gothic construction was a perfect blending of unusual creativity and clear form. The form came from clear structural demands, and the creativity was inventiveness and flair.

As we have seen, the Gothic builders sought to give the impression of a church that soars into the sky, higher than had previously been imaginable, symbolic of the connection between heaven and earth. To do this, they employed vaults, arches and clerestory windows – all of which had been in use since the invention of the first Roman basilica. A vault is a method of raising a roof, simply put, and the semicircular or 'barrel' vaults of Romanesque churches did not create enough of a soaring effect to satisfy the Gothic imagination. As one recent writer has explained it, 'The classic Romanesque arch is a smooth semicircle made from blocks stacked into a crescent. It is not the mortar that is primarily responsible for holding these stones together, but their pressure against one another.'[3] Pointed or 'ribbed' vaults were used, instead. As a result, gravity worked against this new form, rather than along with it. Meanwhile, clerestory, or 'clear storey', windows are those that are above the roof line created by the nave and aisles of a church; by definition, these windows are above eye-level, intended to light an area rather than to create a view. Both vaults and windows grew larger and larger in Gothic constructions. With ribbed vaulting, good masonry alone could not support the new height.

A buttress, simply put, is a support to a vaulted wall. It extends from the wall of a chapel or cloister to somewhere outside the building, propping it up. The most rudimentary buttress, created since buildings were first built, is a perpendicular or simply vertical support that touches the outside of a wall at one end, and rests on the ground, at the other. The walls of Gothic cathedrals, however, were made particularly weak by a thinner use of stone in an effort to reach higher and higher, and the multiplied use of many windows to allow lots of light in. A different or more complete buttress system was required, and it had to match the upwardness of the cathedral design.

> Some flying buttress designs are enormously exciting, but the flying buttress originates as an awkwardness, a structural necessity imposed by the ambitions of the interior. (Richard Jenkyns)[4]

The Gothic builders added some creative flair to their buttresses. They caused a buttress to *fly* by adding an arch to it, making it an aspect of the beauty of the outside of the building, rather than something purely structural. Earlier builders had always hidden their buttresses – they were viewed as a sign of weakness in a building – but the Gothic sensibility was to make that weakness into a piece of beauty. During the Gothic Revival in England, Pugin once famously ridiculed St Paul's Cathedral for having concealed, rather than flying, buttresses, and for having 'a fictitious dome' – the dome that is seen from the outside is only for decoration. Every element should be both functional and beautiful, Pugin believed, and the Gothic style was to take pride in the way that buttresses fly.

Building flying buttresses was an integrated process that began when the nave and transepts were going up. In order to build one it was common for carpenters to hoist wooden frames that would help to hold the stone walls in place, despite the pressure on them to fold outwards. These frames would help hold things together until much heavier mortar and stone could replace them. Over time, they became more and more decorative and ornamental, sometimes with many tiers, and sometimes it seems that those additional tiers were not even necessary from an engineering point of view. Often criticized as a crude addition to an otherwise practical art form, the flying buttress, since it is a structural support that goes unhidden, is yet another sign that the builders wanted the structure to soar.

The Gothic moment of the twelfth and thirteenth centuries was the first time that the flying buttress was embraced. The Gothic builders believed that they were essential to the message of the church. Soaring height has a theological aim. They were devoted to height that seemed unreasonable in its time. In fact, that cranky theologian, Bernard of Clairvaux, spent a lot of energy criticizing height even before the great Gothic cathedrals were underway. In 1124, a little more than a decade before Abbot Suger began the reconstruction of the Abbey Church of St-Denis (and seventy years before the new Chartres was underway), Bernard complained that his own Order's architecture was getting out of hand. The Romanesque style used in Cistercian churches was becoming too extravagant for his tastes, as he criticized 'the measureless height of the houses of prayer, their exaggerated length, their useless width, the amount of stonemasons' work they involve, their paintings which stimulate curiosity and disturb prayer'.[5]

> Gothic is less a method of construction, than it is a mental attitude, the visualizing of a spiritual impulse.
> (Ralph Adams Cram)

The great nineteenth-century art critic, John Ruskin, was of the school that says that the builders would have concealed their buttresses if they were able. The outside of the cath-

edral is 'the wrong side,' he said, 'in which you find out how
the threads go that produce the inside, or right side, pattern.'[6]
I think that Ruskin was missing something, here. You won't
ultimately be able to grasp the spiritual perspective of flying buttresses unless you walk around the area outside of
a Gothic cathedral before going in. The 'front' door of a
cathedral is almost always the western portal. Laid out to
resemble a cross (when seen from above), the longer axis of
a cathedral runs from west to east, and the east end is where
the altar is located. The west end is the front door. But in
order to get the proper understanding, it is best to walk around
the perimeter of the building.

As you walk around outside, recognize the presence of the
nave and the aisles, and see how (in most cases) the outside
of the nave is full of flying buttresses. At Chartres Cathedral,
for instance, the nave rises twice as high – maybe more – as
the aisles themselves. This is intentional. The nave is the primary place for the people of God, all of them, and the flying
buttresses symbolize our desires and efforts to be there,
allowing Christ to win us back for heaven.

> To death condemned by awful sentence,
> God recalled us to repentance,
>   Sending His only Son;
> Whom He loved He came to cherish;
> Whom His justice doomed to perish,
>   By grace to life he won.
> Infinity, Immensity,
> Whom no human eye can see
>   Or human thought contain,
> Made of infinity a space,
> Made of Immensity a place,
>   To win us Life again.
>   (Adam of St Victor)[7]

I sometimes imagine that flying buttresses are like holy fools: their purpose and value are rarely grasped in time. Their method is the large part of their message. When Francis of Assisi heard the voice of God in his soul, telling him to 'Go and rebuild my church' – he heard it simply, without any grandeur whatever. He gathered stones and went to work on strengthening the structure of San Damiano, the little church where he had heard the message. But still, there was plenty of bling to Francis' methods. He was extravagant in his devotion to God, and unwittingly clever in his passion. As a fool for Christ, he often played the fool himself, demonstrating his love for God and relative disregard for the values of the world (decorum, property, honour) in ways that caused others to notice what he was about. Francis liked to think of himself and his first friars as 'God's jugglers' who would travel from village to village in Italy and elsewhere entertaining people with the good news. The earliest Franciscans begged for their bread, often slept outdoors, and spent a lot of time with lepers – who at that time were complete outcasts of both society and Church. In those days, their actions were deemed bizarre, and the children of the villages would often throw mud at the crazy friars, treating them as being as low on the social scale as vagabond lunatics. For Francis, however, deliberate simplicity had a purpose in ministry. He and the first Franciscans were aiming to distinguish themselves clearly from the institutional Church and the wealthy religious Orders of their day. As a result, so many men and women soon wanted to join Francis that he was forced to create what he called the 'Third Order', giving laypeople a way to join the spirit and efforts of the Franciscan movement without leaving family, job or community.

Flying buttresses had similar effects in the thirteenth and fourteenth centuries – they distinguished the Gothic style in ways that caused people to notice the bigger purpose of a cathedral. Like grotesques, they were a way of balancing the riches inside the cathedral with an extravagant message on the outside. They revitalized the outside of buildings that are designed only to draw you in.

9

Beauty awakens belief

I'm not an art critic or an aesthete. There was a time not long ago when a book such as this one would be described as contributing to the 'history of taste'. That's not my intention at all. I am a reader, a writer and a pilgrim. I am drawn to beauty, to God and to churches, and these form a trinity of meaning in Gothic cathedrals. There is more to beauty than meets the eye, and by rediscovering the medieval attitude toward beauty, it is possible to repurpose cathedrals for today, and to have a cathedral spirituality, today.

'Beauty is for the bourgeois,' says the character Tolya Sukhanov in Olga Grushin's 2005 novel, *The Dream Life of Sukhanov*,[1] echoing a popular theme in western culture. Grushin's Tolya promptly puts the lovely book of Botticelli, that he adores, away. He'll no longer permit himself to enjoy it. Am I supposed to feel guilty that I love the adornments of Gothic churches? I don't think so. The issues are more complicated than that. We need to reclaim what beauty means for our lives.

I didn't write this book because I believe that the Gothic style is the only one that is authentically Christian. Those arguments were for the Gothic Revival of the nineteenth century. Augustus Welby Pugin (who designed Birmingham Cathedral, the Houses of Parliament in Westminster, and many other buildings) argued these principles most strenuously. He said,

The Greeks erected their columns like the uprights of Stonehenge, just so far apart that the blocks they laid on them would not break by their own weight. The Christian architects, on the contrary [Pugin was always contrasting the 'Greek' or 'ancient' architects with the 'Christian' or 'Gothic' ones], during the dark ages, with stone scarcely larger than ordinary bricks, threw their lofty vaults from slender pillars across a vast intermediate space, and that at an amazing height, where they had every difficulty of lateral pressure to contend with.[2]

The era of moralizing about why one architectural style is better than another is gratefully past. Rediscovering medieval attitudes toward beauty in God does not have to mean these sorts of harsh judgements.

Imagine that you woke up one morning and every great cathedral was vanished from the face of the earth, as in a science fiction novel or film.

One of the most intriguing stories that Graham Greene ever wrote is also one of his least known. It is called 'The Last Word' and was published for the first time in 1988, near the end of Greene's life. It tells a futuristic story of the last pope, long after the Catholic Church and all other churches have ceased to exist. He is called by the General, the man who now runs the World Government, for a final meeting.

At the beginning of the story, the old man barely remembers that 25 December is Christmas Day. He is told that Christmas was abolished more than twenty years before. As the narrator tells it, 'He was left wondering – how does one abolish a day?' The old man is told that someone will pick him up at the airport on that day to take him to see the General.

Before they meet, the pope is asked to dress in his uniform. 'My uniform?' he asks, unsure of what that might mean.

But then he discovers clothing that he only vaguely remembers, and one of the assistants reminds him, 'You were a priest. These robes have been lent by the World Museum of Myths for the occasion.'

While meeting with the General, Pope John (he learns that that was once his name) is told by the General: 'You are the last living Christian. You are a historic figure . . . I expect you were a good pope as popes go, and I want to do you the honour of no longer keeping you in these dreary conditions.'

The aim of this fateful meeting is for the General to shoot the last pope dead, putting an end to what had already ended in every other respect long beforehand. '*Corpus Domini nostri* . . .' the pope begins to say, as if from some long-ago memory, just as the gun is fired. These are the words from the Tridentine Mass: '*Corpus Domini nostri* . . .' (May the Body of Our Lord . . . Jesus Christ keep my soul unto life everlasting. Amen.) Ominously, Greene's last paragraph goes like this: 'Between the pressure on the trigger and the bullet exploding a strange and frightening doubt crossed his mind: is it possible that what this man believed may be true?'[3]

Greene's futuristic tale hasn't come true, and surely never will. But in the near future, if not already, the Christian world will be so thoroughly post-Christian that this sort of story becomes more conceivable.

The great cathedrals are symbols of a past that once was. They are symbols that can come alive again, because what they mean is essential for what the world needs. The cathedrals that we have explored in this book tell a certain narrative about what it means to be alive, to be human, and to relate to God and others. They were also intended to create a new expression of church – and of Church. We no longer believe these things as the people of the Gothic era once did. The soaring, towering, luminous, contemplatively light-and-dark images of cathedrals make less sense to us than they did to our ancestors. But that doesn't mean we cannot rediscover the spirituality that made sense then, and still makes sense today.

One recent morning in my book group in Vermont, we were all discussing the subject of happiness. 'When was the last time that you experienced true joy?' someone asked. I had to think about it for a while, and while I did, each person in the group took turns with a story or experience.

'I remember once climbing to the top of a mountain, and as I stood there in the open air the sun began to set, and I felt joy,' one person said.

Another explained, 'I remember riding a pony each summer as a girl, with the wind in my hair. I think that I felt joy most of all, at those times.'

And then others described experiences on the ocean or somewhere else in nature. Meanwhile, I sat in my chair nonplussed. I had no similar accounts to offer. I couldn't think of a single time that I had experienced true joy. Could this be true? Is my life really that sad?

But then I realized: I was having difficulty answering the question because everyone else in my book group answered it from a singular perspective. I realized that I don't usually feel joy all alone, and I don't often feel joy in nature, as others do. Instead, I feel joy most often in crowds of people: in the middle of Times Square on a Friday night, or at a packed football game, or in a crowded orchestra hall, or in the sound of hundreds of feet shuffling behind me as we all walk forward for Communion. I said this out loud to my group.

One of the older women replied,

You know, now that you mention it, I have felt that way, too. A few months ago, my daughter took me to a hockey game in Boston. I never go to hockey games, but I went, because she wanted to. We were sitting up close, right in front of the glass. There were three young men, my daughter's age, sitting in the row beside us. They were drinking beer after beer and constantly begging our pardon to shuffle past and exit to the toilets. Then they'd come back and step on our toes again, as they took their seats. And then they'd order more beers, and so on and on it went. It was hot in there, and I was sweating all night long. The game was very close, although I understood little of what was going on. In the final period, our team tied the score and then it went into overtime. In overtime, we won at the last possible moment and the entire stadium erupted with excitement. One of those three guys who had annoyed us all night grabbed me and hugged me; another one hugged my daughter. We were jumping up and down. It was as if everyone was one at that moment.

'Yes,' she said, 'I really felt joy that night.'

That hockey arena created the experience of a medieval cathedral for my book group friend. This is one of the most essential meanings of a great cathedral – they are sacred spaces intended to hold entire towns. There, my meaning in life is the same as yours; we are dependent and intimately related to one another.

It is common today for historians of church architecture to characterize the Gothic moment as aimed only at transcendent values, while most modern styles (the sorts of churches that have been built in the last half-century) are more helpfully immanent.[4] These experts sometimes argue that while the Gothic aimed to point people toward God's transcendent otherness, instilling reverence in those who worship, the modern aims to redirect the focus on the people of God and the work of God, instead. The distinction makes *some* sense – the Gothic style certainly aims the senses upward toward heaven – but the value judgement it makes is incorrect. The purpose of a late medieval church used to be to serve its parish, all of the people in its area. People didn't shop from one church to the next. Belonging was the point of being there; belonging to other people, to a community, to neighbours, to God.

Perhaps I'm only yearning for a distant Catholic past when faith was more expansive, and faith's expressions were more local. When belonging wasn't defined by belief, and cathedrals (just like churches, in general) made sense in people's lives. When I stand in a space like Chartres Cathedral today, I imagine crowds of people. What football stadiums look like, today, the cathedrals looked like centuries ago: brimming with humanity. The paintings of Brueghel imagine these scenes. But the Gothic moment came to a close when Christians began to change the story of God's relationship to humanity to one of fear rather than creation. And the belief that God resided in the cathedral, or that God could be found there in any special way, began to fall away in the decades leading up to the Renaissance and the Reformation. People began a new course of enlightenment, a modern way that left behind much. Christian spirituality took an inward turn from which it has never recovered, and the Gothic cathedrals slowly became memories rather than active places of worship and everyday life. When it really comes down to it, I guess that my love for the great Gothic cathedrals is the same as my desire for one body, one Church.

The Church as monastery and cathedral

Monastery and *cathedral* are two more metaphors that Christians have used to understand the world, and that help to explain the basic differences between the Romanesque and Gothic, or between Mont St-Michel and Chartres.

The monastery – and Mont St-Michel represents this perfectly – stands alone, as a message to the world about what is most true and essential. The cathedral, on the other hand, stands to transform its surroundings; it wants to be at the centre, and to put religion in its proper place at the centre of people's lives. As art historian, Michael Camille, once wrote: 'Unlike the monastery, which was opposed to the world, the cathedral stood within clamorous streets, a powerful symbol of God's expanding business among the rising urban communities of the thirteenth century.'[5]

Every great church, regardless of its architectural style, represents our desire to be with God. The Abbey of Mont St-Michel stands in stark contrast to the Jacob's Ladder of Chartres Cathedral. The images are apt: Mont St-Michel is the symbol of Christian strength that once was. While the Mont rests in shallow and strange waters, Chartres Cathedral soars in the centre of town. Where Mont St-Michel represents the withdrawal from society in order to seek salvation, Chartres is the redeeming of society and secular life. Mont St-Michel is massive, fortified, isolated, withdrawn and militant; while Chartres is soaring, palatial, central, communal and aesthetic. I discovered parts of my own spiritual make-up in both places, under the umbrella of both sets of metaphors.

Some portions of Scripture spoke profoundly to the architects that set out to redesign Romanesque sanctuaries, chancels and naves into Gothic ones. We know that Psalm 48, for instance, inspired them. The image of *cathedral* became a primary symbol – an instructional, sacred space – modelled after the ideal of a New Jerusalem:

> Great is the LORD and greatly to be praised
>   in the city of our God.
> His holy mountain, beautiful in elevation,
>   is the joy of all the earth.
> Mount Zion, in the far north,
>   the city of the great King.
> Within its citadels God
>   has shown himself a sure defence . . .

as when an east wind shatters
   the ships of Tarshish.
As we have heard, so have we seen
   in the city of the Lord of hosts,
in the city of our God,
   which God establishes for ever . . .
   Let Mount Zion be glad,
let the towns of Judah rejoice
   because of your judgements.
Walk about Zion, go all around it,
   count its towers,
consider well its ramparts;
   go through its citadels,
that you may tell the next generation.
            (Psalm 48.1–3, 7–8, 11–13)

This New Jerusalem was also foretold in the Apocalypse of St John, reminding medieval Christians of the holy tabernacle to be rebuilt at the end of the ages. The Gothic builders saw *cathedral* in passages such as this one, more than they saw *monastery*:

And I saw the holy city, the new Jerusalem, coming down out of heaven from God, prepared as a bride adorned for her husband. And I heard a loud voice from the throne saying,

'See, the home of God is among mortals.
He will dwell with them;
they will be his peoples,
and God himself will be with them;
he will wipe every tear from their eyes.
Death will be no more;
mourning and crying and pain will be no more,
for the first things have passed away.'

... Then one of the seven angels ... showed me the holy
city Jerusalem coming down out of heaven from God.
It has the glory of God and a radiance like a very rare
jewel, like jasper, clear as crystal. It has a great, high wall
with twelve gates, and at the gates twelve angels, and on
the gates are inscribed the names of the twelve tribes
of the Israelites; on the east three gates, on the north
three gates, on the south three gates, and on the west
three gates. And the wall of the city has twelve foundations, and on them are the twelve names of the
twelve apostles of the Lamb ... The wall is built of
jasper, while the city is pure gold, clear as glass. The foundations of the wall of the city are adorned with every
jewel ... And the twelve gates are twelve pearls, each of
the gates is a single pearl, and the street of the city is
pure gold, transparent as glass. I saw no temple in the
city, for its temple is the Lord God the Almighty and
the Lamb. And the city has no need of sun or moon to
shine on it, for the glory of God is its light, and its lamp
is the Lamb. The nations will walk by its light, and the
kings of the earth will bring their glory into it. Its gates
will never be shut by day – and there will be no night
there.   (Revelation 21.2–4, 9–13, 18–19, 21–25)

A journey from Mont St-Michel to Chartres can be spiritually dizzying, but only because these two places represent such
profound aspects of what it means to be in the presence of
God.

I would like to see what I imprecisely call 'a return to cathedral spirituality'. The enormous space of the great Gothic
churches, like stadiums, direct our attention to the *crowd of
God*. Like the rose window, modelled after a worldview that
saw the entire universe held in one tight circle, cathedrals
are enactments of the way that everyone and everything is

included in God's path. Perhaps cathedrals are more ideal for the postmodern world than they even were for the pre-modern one in which they were first built. Whereas the modern people of God can be like an exclusive club, the post-modern *crowd of God* is those of all backgrounds and dispositions who come in and out of the great cathedrals throughout the world. The combination of intimacy and anonymity that such places are designed to foster means that we benefit from them without even knowing it. You don't have to be a member of any church in order to experience what the Gothic builders intended. Cathedral spirituality is about experiencing God's presence with other people.

The Gothic cathedral was a new expression of church for the twelfth and thirteenth centuries, welcoming the Church, all people, to fill its naves with every manner of human activity. The elements of cathedral spirituality are intellectual, incarnational and even kinaesthetic – in reverse order. Kinaesthetically we experience the stone, light and height with our senses, almost in the way that one feels exercise. Incarnationally we experience the images of Christ and Mary and all of the saints, seeing how they sought holiness in human frailty. And intellectually we ask questions, study and learn the more subtle ways that the medieval imagination wants to teach us about the story of God.

> The Church was God, and its lines excluded interference. God and the Church embraced all the converging lines of the universe, and the universe showed none but lines that converged. Between God and Man, nothing whatever intervened.
>
> (Henry Adams, *Mont Saint Michel and Chartres*)[6]

Toward the end of my recent trip in northern France, I noticed an elderly man, probably in his eighties, walking in and out of a church in Brittany, over and over again, carrying handfuls of fresh flowers. He must have walked past me eight or nine times during the hour or two that I was visiting that particular church. He would carry flowers in and place them in vases on the altars of certain side chapels. I watched him while he gently dusted off the statuary. A couple of other times, he was carrying boxes of candles and other things in and out of the building.

This little man looked like a French peasant – the sort of man I had read about in François Mauriac novels and W. S. Merwin memoirs – and had a full head of white hair. This particular church that he was caring for was far off the tourist path. Its timbered roof was illuminated in places by exposed light bulbs hanging down. But it was well loved in other ways, including the flowers in the chapels. On the walls of some of those chapels – not only in this Brittany church but throughout rural areas of northern France – are small ceramic plaques often with a single word painted upon them: MERCI. On one chapel wall, I saw three plaques, surely paid for and put there by three different recipients of answered prayers over the years, and they read, MERCI, MERCI 1893, and then a simple MERCI, again.

Sometimes it is these out-of-the-way churches, the ones that rarely appear on travel itineraries, that are the most enjoyable. Like the Gothic churches that represent a variety of centuries, taking on the personality of its parish during each successive century, churches like this charming one in Brittany might be compared to a hymn book. Built upon the riches of ancient texts, as well as some tunes that are almost as old, they also include the adornments of each century and generation as it attempts to remain faithful to its foundations.

This elderly man's eyes were lively but they did not meet my own, at least not while we were inside. Sometime later, as I was outside the church walking around its perimeter and admiring the carvings, statues and gargoyles, the man was outside and standing beside what was obviously his bicycle.

He was about to remove it from its stand and climb aboard when he stopped and looked at me.

'Bum ba bum ba bum *que tu* bum ba *église* bum bum?' I heard him say (I understand very little French), a large smile spread across his face. I turned and met his smile.

'I am sorry . . . don't speak *Français*,' I replied, with a look of apology. I am accustomed to looking this way whenever I'm with French-speaking people.

He began again, 'Umm . . . no *Français* . . .' those eyes searching heavenward for words perhaps not spoken for a very long time, 'You like . . . umm . . . this church. Umm . . . I know all of this church. It is part of me, and I, it. So, you ask me anything,' he said, smiling even more broadly.

I loved that.

Notes

1 The worldview of the Gothic cathedral

1 Johann Herder, in *The Literary Background of the Gothic Revival in Germany*, ed. W. D. Robson-Scott; Oxford: Clarendon Press, 1965; 66.

2 Georges Duby, *The Age of Cathedrals: Art and Society, 980–1420*; trans. Eleanor Levieux and Barbara Thompson; Chicago: University of Chicago Press, 1983; 157.

3 W. H. Auden, in *Modern Canterbury Pilgrims*, ed. James A. Pike; New York: Morehouse-Gorham, 1956; 33–4.

2 Inviting God in: space

1 E. H. Gombrich, *The Story of Art: Pocket Edition*; New York: Phaidon, 2006; 141–2.

2 Henry Adams, *Mont Saint Michel and Chartres*; New York: Penguin Books, 1986; 37. All subsequent quotations from Henry Adams will be from this edition.

3 Ken Follett, *The Pillars of the Earth*; London: Pan Books, 2007; viii.

4 Eric Gill, *Beauty Looks After Herself*; New York: Sheed & Ward, 1933; 66–7.

5 Pope Benedict XVI, *Deus Caritas Est*, 25 December 2005; paragraph 14.

6 Sebastien Roulliard, in *Chartres Cathedral*, ed. Robert Branner; New York: W. W. Norton, 1996; 105.

7 Gill, *Beauty*, 53.

3 Making our places holy: sanctuary

1 Herder, *Literary Background*, 71.

2 Otto von Simson, *The Gothic Cathedral: Origins of Gothic Architecture and the Medieval Concept of Order*; Princeton, NJ: Princeton University Press, 1988; 163.

3 Victor Hugo, *Notre-Dame of Paris*; book 3, chapter 1. This novel first appeared in French in 1831, and has been published in hundreds of editions in English.

4 Thomas Aquinas, quoted in Erwin Panofsky, *Gothic Architecture and Scholasticism*; New York: The New American Library, 1957; 38.

5 Von Simson, *Gothic Cathedral*, 167.

6 Hugo, *Notre-Dame*, book 5, chapter 2.

7 Quoted by Phoebe Stanton, *Pugin*; New York: The Viking Press, 1971; 76.

8 Tertullian, quoted in D. R. Dendy, *The Use of Lights in Christian Worship*; London: SPCK, 1959; 2.

9 Erwin Panofsky, *Abbot Suger on the Abbey Church of Saint-Denis and Its Treasures*; 2nd edn by Gerda Panofsky-Soergel; Princeton: Princeton University Press, 1979; 25.

10 Abbot Suger, in Panofsky, *Abbot Suger*, 63–5.

11 Abbot Suger, in Panofsky, *Abbot Suger*, 65.

12 William Blake, *The Letters of William Blake*, ed. Geoffrey Keynes; Cambridge: Harvard University Press, 1970; 30. Blake's eccentric capitalizations and punctuations have been standardized.

13 Abbot Suger, in Panofsky, *Abbot Suger*, 59.

14 Abbot Suger, quoted in Anselme Dimier, *Stones Laid Before the Lord: Architecture and Monastic Life*, trans. Gilchrist Lavigne; Kalamazoo, MI: Cistercian Publications, 1999; 171.

15 Panofsky, *Abbot Suger*, 47, 49.

16 'Deportations and Families', *Catholic Worker*, vol. LXXIV, no. 7, December 2007; 1.

17 *Spe Salvi*, paragraph 48.

4 A place that is cool: stone

1 Annie Dillard, *Teaching a Stone to Talk: Expeditions and Encounters*, rev. edn; New York: Harper Perennial, 1988; 52.

2 Jean Gimpel, *The Cathedral Builders*; New York: Grove Press, 1983; 1.

3 G. H. Cook, *The English Mediaeval Parish Church*; London: Phoenix House, 1954; 207–8.

4 Raymond P. Rhinehart, *Princeton University*; New York: Princeton Architectural Press, 1999; 134.

5 Cecil Headlam, *The Story of Chartres*; London: J. M. Dent & Co., 1902; 117.

6 Pseudo-Dionysius, in *The Origins of the Christian Mystical Tradition: From Plato to Denys*, Andrew Louth; New York: Oxford University Press, 1983; 167–8.

5 Open your eyes and see: light

1 John McGahern, *All Will Be Well: A Memoir*; New York: Vintage Books, 2007; 215.

2 Father Matt Torpley, OCSO, in conversation with the author, 7 September 2002.

3 Jean Verdon, *Night in the Middle Ages*, trans. George Holoch; Notre Dame, IN: University of Notre Dame Press, 2002; 71.

4 Bernard of Clairvaux, quoted in C. H. Lawrence, *Medieval Monasticism*; Harlow, Essex: Longman, 1984; 154.

5 Augustine, *Confessions*, VII, 9–10.

6 Plotinus, *The Enneads*, 3rd edn, trans. Stephen MacKenna; London: Faber & Faber, 1962; 617.

7 Duby, *Age of Cathedrals*, 100.

8 Panofsky, *Abbot Suger*, 55.

9 *The Essence of Plotinus: Extracts from the Six Enneads and Porphyry's Life of Plotinus*, compiled by Grace H. Turnbull; New York: Oxford University Press, 1934; 118.

10 Quoted in Panofsky, *Abbot Suger*, 20.

6 Learning to live with the light off: darkness

1 Pseudo-Dionysius the Areopagite, *Mystical Theology*, ch. 1. Translation mine.

2 *The Essence of Plotinus*, 122.

3 Adams, *Mont Saint Michel*, 138–9.

4 St John of the Cross, *The Complete Works of St John of the Cross*, 3 vols, trans. and ed. E. Allison Peers; Westminster, MD: The Newman Press, 1953; I, 325, 356.

5 St John of the Cross, *The Ascent of Mount Carmel*, chapter 9, paragraph 3. Various editions; translation mine.

7 Don't take yourself too seriously: gargoyles

1 Eric Gill, *Last Essays*; London: Jonathan Cape, 1942; 18.
2 John Ruskin, from 'The Nature of Gothic', a chapter in *The Stones of Venice*. See John Ruskin, *Unto This Last and Other Writings*, ed. Clive Wilmer; New York: Penguin Books, 1985; 79.
3 Wilhelm Voge, in *Chartres Cathedral*, ed. Robert Branner; New York: W. W. Norton, 1996; 229–30.
4 Gill, *Last Essays*, 9.
5 Henri Focillon, in Branner, *Chartres Cathedral*, 191.
6 Dante, *Inferno* VII, 122–5, from *The Comedy of Dante Alighieri the Florentine: Hell*, trans. Dorothy L. Sayers; Harmondsworth, Middlesex: Penguin Books, 1949.
7 Augustine of Hippo, *The City of God*, vol. 2; trans. John Healey, ed. R. V. G. Tasker; New York: Everyman's Library, 1945; book XVI, chapter viii, 107.
8 Hugo, *Notre-Dame*, book 5, chapter 2.
9 Michael Camille, *Image on the Edge: The Margins of Medieval Art*; Cambridge, MA: Harvard University Press, 1992; 9.
10 Emile Male, *The Gothic Image: Religious Art in France of the Thirteenth Century*; New York: Harper Torchbooks, 1958; 60.

8 Reaching to heaven: flying buttresses

1 Quoted in Stanton, *Pugin*, 85.
2 Panofsky, *Abbot Suger*, 65.
3 Philip Ball, *Universe of Stone: Chartres Cathedral and the Triumph of the Medieval Mind*; London: The Bodley Head, 2008; 201.
4 Richard Jenkyns, *Westminster Abbey*; Cambridge, MA: Harvard University Press, 2005; 15.
5 Bernard of Clairvaux, quoted in Ball, *Universe of Stone*, 27.
6 John Ruskin, quoted in Ball, *Universe of Stone*, 27.
7 Adam of St Victor, quoted in Adams, *Mont Saint Michel*, 308.

9 Beauty awakens belief

1 Olga Grushin, *The Dream Life of Sukhanov*; New York: Putnam, 2006; 93.
2 Augustus Welby Pugin, *True Principles of Pointed or Christian Architecture*, 1841; lecture 1.

3 Graham Greene, *The Last Word and Other Stories*; New York: Penguin Books, 1992; 3–18.

4 For one recent example, see Mark A. Torgerson, *An Architecture of Immanence: Architecture for Worship and Ministry Today*; Grand Rapids, MI: Eerdmans, 2007.

5 Camille, *Image*, 77.

6 Adams, *Mont Saint Michel*, 337.